Advance Praise for

The Trouble with School Behavior and Discipline Policies in Neoliberal Times

"This important book reminds education scholars that the political remains entrenched with/in the personal. Extending a tradition of reflexive critical inquiry into the social politics of schooling and systemic education, Robinson poses important new questions for considering pedagogical practice and our work as educators. Using personal accounts and reflections of everyday classroom encounters interwoven with adept applications of the critical education literature, Robinson demonstrates her positioning at the center of current debates surrounding the purpose of education. This book is both a reminder of what is at stake in schooling, and a clarion for creating new educational imaginaries."
—Andrew Hickey, Professor, School of Humanities and Communication,
University of Southern Queensland

"Robinson's account of the 'trouble' with school discipline and behavior is honest and unflinching in its examination of the disconnection between the lives of young people and the policies and practices designed to coerce, control and manage them. Drawing together rich theorisations and confronting empirical evidence from her work in Western Australian schools, Robinson shines a light on the harmful 'common sense' of school discipline policies and practices, pointing towards the possibilities of a more relational and democratic schooling for all young people."
—Stewart Riddle, Professor (Curriculum & Pedagogy), School of Education,
University of Southern Queensland

The *Trouble* with School Behavior and Discipline Policies in Neoliberal Times

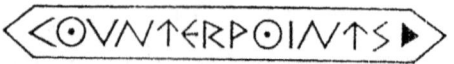

Shirley R. Steinberg
Series Editor

Vol. 556

New York - Berlin - Bruxelles - Chennai - Lausanne - Oxford

Janean Robinson

The *Trouble* with School Behavior and Discipline Policies in Neoliberal Times

New York · Berlin · Bruxelles · Chennai · Lausanne · Oxford

Library of Congress Cataloging-in-Publication Data

Names: Robinson, Janean, author.
Title: The *trouble* with school behavior and discipline policies in neoliberal times / Janean Robinson.
Description: New York, NY: Peter Lang, 2025. | Series: Counterpoints, 1058–1634; Volume 556 | Includes bibliographical references and index.
Identifiers: LCCN 2024036582 (print) | LCCN 2024036583 (ebook) | ISBN 9781636673325 (hardback) | ISBN 9781636673295 (paperback) | ISBN 9781636673301 (pdf) | ISBN 9781636673318 (epub)
Subjects: LCSH: School discipline. | Neoliberalism. | Behavior modification. | School management and organization. | School discipline–Western Australia–Case studies. | Education and state.
Classification: LCC LB3012 .R63 2025 (print) | LCC LB3012 (ebook) | DDC 371.54–dc23/eng/20240819
LC record available at https://lccn.loc.gov/2024036582
LC ebook record available at https://lccn.loc.gov/2024036583
DOI 10.3726/b22338

Bibliographic information published by the Deutsche Nationalbibliothek.
The German National Library lists this publication in the German National Bibliography; detailed bibliographic data is available on the Internet at http://dnb.d-nb.de.

Cover design by Peter Lang Group AG

ISSN 1058-1634 (print)
ISBN 9781636673295 (paperback)
ISBN 9781636673325 (hardback)
ISBN 9781636673301 (ebook)
ISBN 9781636673318 (epub)
DOI 10.3726/b22338

© 2025 Peter Lang Group AG, Lausanne
Published by Peter Lang Publishing Inc., New York, USA

info@peterlang.com—www.peterlang.com

All rights reserved.
All parts of this publication are protected by copyright.
Any utilization outside the strict limits of the copyright law, without the permission of the publisher, is forbidden and liable to prosecution.
This applies in particular to reproductions, translations, microfilming, and storage and processing in electronic retrieval systems.

This publication has been peer reviewed.

This book is dedicated to Emeritus Professor Barry Down, the greatest mentor and 'living legend' one could ever wish for in guiding the path on which to travel to write this book.

TABLE OF CONTENTS

	Acknowledgments	ix
Chapter 1	*Troubling* School Behavior and Discipline Policies: Critical Moments, and "just" Research	1
Chapter 2	The Broader Educational Policy Landscape	19
Chapter 3	The Troubling and Cyclic Historical Context	37
Chapter 4	Heron High: Case Study One	63
Chapter 5	Anchorage High: Case Study Two	81
Chapter 6	Hope for Transformation: Finding the Relational	103
Chapter 7	Conclusion: Schooling *for* Democracy (Riddle, 2022)	115
	Index	127

ACKNOWLEDGMENTS

When I reflect on who I wish to thank for assisting me in creating this book, I return to those memories of adults who taught me the values of social justice, respect for others, fairness and accommodating difference. These were the teachers who took the time to understand the child, even when the child was either too restless or too still.

These were also the teachers that engaged and motivated me in my journey as secondary school teacher and later as academic and research scholar. Significant mentors and role models in this journey include John Smyth, Peter McInerney and Robert Hattam, whose dedication to social justice advocacy and activism in school and community renewal have not only been inspirational but have also shown that change is indeed possible during neoliberal times. These are the wise "elders" of my journey. The "young(er)" gurus who have connected us all and continued to show me the way have included Stewart Riddle and Andrew Hickey, whose dedication to reclaiming the relational and continual drive *for* democracy provide hope for education into the future.

The School Exclusions Policy and Practice research team, Education Futures, University South Australia, have provided essential support to continue researching within the educational field of school behavior and discipline. I thank Jamie Manolev for recommending contemplating writing a book all that time ago, and I thank Anna Sullivan for leading and keeping our team "on task" toward completion of this important project that I know will have national and international impact.

I also wish to acknowledge teaching colleagues and those students I interviewed from both case study schools who provided the stories to bring their own understandings, experiences, insights and versions of school managerial reform and discipline policy enactments; from the classrooms, into the world, for others to be informed. I am confident that these voices will resonate and linger in shaking things up for a long while.

Barry Down has been my greatest mentor of all time. He has been patient, professional and encouraging since the very first tutorial of his I attended in 1995. I was not keen to participate in the compulsory units required for completing the degree that I had delayed and ignored, because in the past, I could find no relevance. I was not interested in history, politics, and critical social theory; and yet these components of that course, and the scholarly and academic journey that Barry continued to mentor, have formed the solid and secure framework of this very book!

Shirley Steinberg has been the radical "big sister" and wise scholar I always wanted in my life and "thank you forever," Barry, for introducing us. Also, thanks to both Barry and Shirley, I now have supportive critical scholars, friends, and families from afar that I continue to be inspired by after meeting them at the 10th Annual Freire Project congress in Bilbao, Spain in 2018.

Barry and the team from Education Futures, University of South Australia also introduced me to my copyeditor, Kate Leeson. I want to sit down and have an appreciative conversation with my new "best friend," Kate, in person, to express my absolute gratitude. I am in awe of her graceful, intuitive, and thorough feedback and expertise.

I would like to thank Alison Jefferson, Joshua Charles and Naviya Palani, editors from Peter Lang Publishers for navigating my manuscript toward final production and of course I am deep in appreciation of Shirley Steinberg, Series Editor, for providing this amazing opportunity to have my work "out there" [keeping] "my inner world awake" (C. W. Mills, 1959, p. 217).

Finally, I acknowledge my dear family and friends who have continued to encourage me to finish the chapters contained within this book over the duration of half my lifetime. I am indebted to you all for your support to have it completed before my 70th birthday party!

· 1 ·

TROUBLING SCHOOL BEHAVIOR AND DISCIPLINE POLICIES: CRITICAL MOMENTS, AND "JUST" RESEARCH

Introduction

This book is animated by the question: why have school behavior and discipline policies become so troubling? As Connell (2013) argues, "in the last few decades, education systems all over the world have been impacted by the rise of neoliberal ideology and practices of government" (p. 99).

In this introductory chapter, I begin to address this question by sharing some personal reflections and critical moments in my professional career as a teacher and researcher. As Giroux (2012) argues, "when institutions of public and higher education have become associated with market competition, conformity, disempowerment, and uncompromising modes of punishment" then it is time to make known "the significant contributions and legacy of Paulo Freire's work" (Giroux, 2012, p. 123). Freire (1992) explains significant critiques are tied to our stories and "what stories we choose to tell, and the way in which we decide to tell them [...] form the provisional basis of what a critical pedagogy of the future might mean" (p. xii). I have selected four of these narratives due to their significance in my teaching and life journey leading to this book. These narratives, which are not presented in chronological order, are titled

"Being Awakened," "Finding Critical Friends," "Creating 'Trouble,'" and "The Personal Becomes Political."

I want this book to be activist in nature, and I declare upfront my scholarly position in this opening chapter. I want to be very clear that I am not neutral, but always positioned as political, both within my research writing and within my practice. This is consistent with my understanding of Freire's legacy. What I continue to learn from Freire is to have the courage to challenge the status quo. In his book, *Pedagogy of the oppressed*, Freire (1970/2005) describes the importance of a critical perception of the world: "which implies a correct method of approaching reality in order to unveil it. And critical perception cannot be imposed. Thus, from the very beginning, thematic investigation is expressed as an educational pursuit, as cultural action" (p. 111).

The third section of this chapter explains *why* school behavior and discipline policies are "troubling" and becomes the focus of critique. I draw on the tradition of critical theory to do this work of interrogating "the trouble," and many contradictions of school discipline. I use theory to help me both unsettle commonsense orthodoxies and search for alternative ways of understanding school discipline. In this manner, the book forms a provisional basis of a critical pedagogy for not only Australian schooling, but for many other schools throughout the world in education systems whose public policies impact in non-democratic and damaging ways on their contemporary and future cultures and societies.

The fourth section of this chapter outlines the kind of research that situates theory within practice by critiquing behavior and discipline policies. This focus leads me to outline the contribution that critical policy ethnography can make, including school-based ethnographies, narratives, and student voice. This section will also briefly outline the case studies of two large government (public) secondary schools in Western Australia that provided the research context of this book.

The final section provides an overview of how the rest of the book is organized.

Critical Moments

Fromm (1956) explains that our society is run by "a managerial bureaucracy, by professional politicians" (p. 197). Presently, within the country in which I was born and spent most of my life (Australia), we have far too many young people turned away, often repeatedly, every single day, from their educational experiences within government (public) schools because they do not perform to a required standard, nor comply, behave, or perform within certain expectations. As Sir Ken Robinson (2013) declared, "education doesn't go on in the committee rooms of legislative buildings; it happens in classrooms and schools and the people who do it are the teachers and the students." For this reason, I want to refer to four critical moments arising from my own journey as a practitioner–researcher as I attempt to comprehend the "trouble" with behavior management and school discipline policies.

Critical Moment 1: Being Awakened

> Whoever teaches learns in the act of teaching, and whoever learns teaches in the act of learning. To learn, then, logically precedes to teach. (Freire, 1998, p. 31)

I had always wanted to be a teacher. In my primary school days as the only female in the final grades in a one-teacher school, I was given the responsible task of sitting with the younger students to read, talk, and stitch together. These were precious moments both for me and for the children. This teaching–learning relationship was not evaluated for standards nor outcomes and yet was appreciated by all those participating. It was a genuine and respectful connection. I was free to be a leader and a learner, and the teacher and parents acknowledged my role.

When completing my qualifying teacher practice in a region many years later at the local high school down the road from this same primary school, I also experienced the community respect and enjoyment of working with young people over a 15-week intense "training on the job." These are also fond memories. I had never heard of Paulo Freire then. I only learnt about Paulo Freire 20 years later in the early 1990s when completing a unit in studies that I had previously avoided: "Policy in Education." I was fortunate to have as my mentor in this unit, Professor Barry Down, who encouraged our graduating group of Bachelor of Education teachers to think and reflect on and about our teaching and our practice in the classrooms we were working within.

Consequently, I and others completing this course were also awakened and relieved to discover that we (as experienced teachers) were not the reason things were becoming so complicated in our classrooms. We also learnt many philosophies and epistemological relationships and terms, including "ideology," "hegemony," "praxis," and "dialogic teaching"—all of which connected to our day-to-day work. We discovered that it was okay to be angry and uncomfortable with some of the unfamiliar reforms we were all experiencing within the schools we were working in and that debate on these issues was welcomed. It was acceptable, therefore, to be critical within our practice of a neoliberal educational system (even if we did not understand it at the time). We also embraced the true meaning of pedagogy as Freire explained it, and we appreciated the space and support to ask difficult and troubling questions—something that had been denied to many of us in our workplaces.

For me personally, having grown up in a conservative, outback, small country town in Western Australia, this was liberating and "heady" fodder to digest and I enthusiastically lapped it up! When encountering these new paradigms as both a practicing and experienced teacher and a keen mature-aged university student, I had much to absorb! Interrogating the power plays and lack of autonomy and challenging the positivist managerial discourse that dominated my workplace, culminated in providing me with the tools and the agency to think and act *otherwise*. The collective struggle and reciprocal support flowed into a "pedagogy of possibility" (Simon, 1992) and consequently I discovered once more that an authentic act of learning within my own practice was indeed possible.

Critical Moment 2: Finding Critical Friends

> Critical teaching [. . .] involves a dynamic and dialectical movement between "doing" and "reflecting on doing." (Freire, 1998, pp. 42–43)

When I returned to teaching in Western Australia in 1994 after a five-year break and living overseas with two young children, I naively thought my 20-year prior experience in the profession was going to make teaching a "walk in the park." However, I quickly realized I was facing a new and shocking reality. I was totally unprepared for the impact that neoliberalism was having around the globe, and specifically for me, within public education. Ball (2021a) describes what had happened whilst I was away from my familiar workplace:

> Schools are being expected to be both innovative and conservative, to deliver both social mobility and social cohesion, to improve both cognitive and non-cognitive skills, to be both collaborative and entrepreneurial. In this sense, education policy as a whole is incoherent and impossible. (p. 210)

I remember viewing a documentary after returning home to Australia titled *The Weather Underground* (Green & Siegel, 2002). This film acknowledged the historical revolution of a group of young Americans who like me opposed war and were practicing social community and activism. What was conflicting for me to understand then, and again now as I write, is that many of these activists were imprisoned for their actions and, even worse, some were killed! Like Freire (1970/2005) this reminds me to reflect on the notion of activism, which will not always be liberating, because activists themselves can be victims of oppression. Instead, Freire argues that true revolution is achieved "with praxis, that is, with *reflection* and *action* directed at the structures to be transformed" (p. 126).

William Ayers was one of the revolutionaries of the Weather Underground who was imprisoned. He particularly inspired me during the viewing because, like me, he was an educator. This was a critical moment for me as I too was an educator struggling to understand the change I was experiencing during this time, and I felt I had discovered an ally in Ayers. Fast forward to the year 2020, I found myself in the fortunate position to be assistant to the editors (Steinberg & Down, 2020) of a significant international critical academic collection on pedagogy, *The Sage handbook of critical pedagogies*. Lo and behold, one of the authors of a chapter in the first section of this collection, "Reading Paulo Freire," was the same activist educator and revolutionary (Ayers, 2020). A passage from his chapter particularly resonated for me because, like him, I also wanted to come together with critical friends by engaging in praxis for revolutionary change:

> the fundamental message of the teacher is this: you can change your life—whoever you are, wherever you've been, whatever you've done, another world is possible. As students and teachers begin to see themselves as linked to one another, as tied to history and capable of collective action, that fundamental message shifts slightly, becoming broader and more generous: we must change ourselves as we come together to change the world. (p. 51)

As well as Ayers, and Freire of course, I am also indebted to the wonderful educators that I have connected with over my lifetime in one way or another and who have continued to inspire and motivate me in my journey of education as liberation and as revolution. That journey is what this book is about; the search for a more humanizing education and asking the question, "how can we do things differently" (Kress, 2011, p. 262). The next section of this chapter will discuss and share some personal reflections regarding the title of this book: *The "trouble" with School Behavior and Discipline Policies in Neoliberal Times*.

Troubling Behavior and Discipline Policies: *Why?* and *How?*

In this section I explain the reasons why "troubling" is so significant in my life and why I have chosen to critique behavior and discipline policies specifically. I begin here by sharing a third critical moment, "Creating *Trouble*."

Critical Moment 3: Creating *Trouble*

> Education is always a certain theory of knowledge put into practice. (Freire, 2004, p. 71)

Firstly, "trouble" appears as a significant phrase in the title of this book for many reasons. From a personal perspective, as a child born in the late 1950s in Australia, I was often considered as a female to be "troublesome." That is, I did not conform to the norms at the time of sitting still and being "good"! Instead, I was regularly caught daydreaming in my own creative outdoor world and refusing indoor quiet time. I was the eldest child in a family with an inherited patriarchal culture, in which my mother was way too busy and too isolated in child-rearing practices to know any alternative. My mother would have been in no position to challenge, let alone question, the archaic, strict, rigid schedules that dominated during the era I was born in nor the social disapproval of excessive affection.

Next, as a primary school student and again a teen in the 1960s and 1970s, I was "in trouble" for questioning anything beyond the traditional in my schooling experiences in remote wheatbelt (farming) towns in Western Australia. As an adult, I was also a problem to be reckoned with when I returned to teach in an overcrowded conservative regional secondary high school in the early 1990s that became entangled in adopting restrictive mandated educational reforms and policies for teachers and students that "troubled" me.

When I persisted then with what I deemed sound pedagogical questions such as *for what, for whom, and why are we doing this?* I was more than often shut down, told to rest, "have a cup of tea," and "get on" with the business of keeping order! I was thus being "systemically silenced" (Kenway, 2011, p. 101). This experience felt not that different from what I had faced as a young child and again as a teenager. Steinberg (2010) explains my experiences as an "insidious kind of trouble" because "you don't know you are in until you are in it" (p. xi). My lived and personal experience of discipline and control, as described by Steinberg, is "a tool of power" because those of us who are continually "in trouble" will continue to be "disciplined" (p. xi).

Why Critique Behavior and Discipline Policies?

I have chosen to critique with fervor the Western Australian Department of Education's evolving behavior and discipline policy, which emerged in 1998 as a major component of the Students at Education Risk Strategy: Making the Difference, and which was also a major strategy of the Plan for Government School Education 1998–2000. This policy was then replaced by the Behavior Management in Schools Policy (WA Department of Education, 1998; WA Department of Education and Training, 2001, 2008), which was then renamed the Student Behavior in Public Schools Policy (WA Department of Education, 2016, 2023). As Ball (2021a) argues, the term policy continues to carry "its own baggage" because "it is an archetypal enlightenment concept" (p. 12).

My compulsion to critique this policy specifically, and the many tensions and contradictions that have consequently unraveled, stems from my firsthand experience of this policy in my own profession as a secondary school teacher, and then again later in researching the impact of the same type of behavior and discipline policies further afield. This form of policy is not only extremely ambiguous in practice, but the unjust and inequitable practices emanating from it are damaging and harmful to many young people. I am, therefore, driven to question, critique, and expose, as I write this book, the insidious and undemocratic practices and procedures occurring, especially in secondary schools, under the guise of *good behavior, positive behavior, quality, standards, improvement,* and *performance*. Kenway and Fahey (2009) name my chosen style of research "defiant" because it "involves questioning received notions and creating new ways of seeing" (p. 14).

I believe there is an urgent need for democratic diversity in educational research and educational practice that is "activist" in nature and demands a disruptive force to contest the power imbalances that presently operate in policy research. This is my "call for the *redistribution* of power" (Biesta et al., 2022, p. 1). It is the students' and many teachers' version of behavior and discipline policy that this book writes *back into* policy research and practice, and it is my conviction that as author I articulate and bring to the fore their stories, especially those struggling in the cultural geography of "the aggressive school" (Smyth & Hattam, 2002, p. 383). I gain courage in the supportive frames of my quest for democracy and social justice, from the collective scholarly wisdom of

Apple et al. (2022) who declare that "education *for* and *as* democracy necessarily involves duty, resistance, creativity, imagination, collective action, and civic courage, which must sit at the heart of any project to reshape societies in the twenty-first century to be more inclusive and sustainable" (p. 247).

How Do I Trouble Behavior and Discipline Discourse?

I begin to trouble behavior and discipline policy discourse by sharing a fourth critical moment in my research journey: "The Personal Becomes Political."

Critical Moment 4: The Personal Becomes Political

> The opposite of education is manipulation, which is based on the absence of faith in the growth of potentialities, and on the conviction that a child will be right only if the adults put into him [sic] what is desirable and suppress what seems to be undesirable. (Fromm, 1956, p. 186)

To provide further context to my choice of policy critique, I reflect on a time in the early 1990s when I had returned to secondary teaching in Western Australia after having lived abroad with my new husband and two young children. I was posted to teach in an overcrowded regional government school that represented everything in polar opposition to that which I had experienced as an eager graduate in 1978. In contrast, teachers were competing and hiding from one another. No-one seemed to want to take responsibility for any action or inaction. There were sirens blaring every hour. The corridors were cold, crowded, and grey. The color and joy in the profession no longer prevailed for me. What was especially concerning was the way in which these tensions and contradictions affected many of the students attending the school I worked in. They too became alienated, bored, and disengaged in learning as the focus turned to regulation, standardization, and top-down control. After twenty years of teaching experience prior to this, I was both shocked and concerned and felt disconnected from this somewhat unfamiliar territory. I therefore found teaching exhausting and unfulfilling because of a culture of survival of the fittest and avoidance of pedagogical obligation and collaboration. This emphasis on being kept busy with performative and accountable tasks, compounded by a lack of confidence, led to a deskilling of our work as teachers (Apple, 2000, p. 116). I also experienced what seemed to me an archaic return to the control and punishment of students and more attention on rewarding compliance. Other more complex interrelations of trust, respect, dignity, appreciation of difference, and the sharing and exploration of ideas and professional resources for the development of knowledge, felt, in comparison, somewhat radical and out of place.

My own performance under this regime, instead of improving as the professional development and performance management packages stated *would* happen, regressed because my working days were reduced to filling out forms and trying to battle through each day. Gunter (2009) re-affirms that my personal teaching experiences and conflicts were legitimately entwined within the political:

> It is a relief to people that they realize that they are not actually responsible for the problems laid upon them. Self-reflexivity also enables people to recognize their achievements in difficult circumstances and work out a sense of self and of the social that can support activism. (p. 100)

I believed then, and still do now, that the role of a teacher of young adults must be reclaimed as one of reciprocal relationship within teaching and learning. This is an "empowering education" (Shor, 1992) for *all*. This is an education and pedagogy that *can* make a difference. This is a *critical* pedagogy, and one that Kress (2020) explains, was Freire's philosophy because it "always starts with the learner as a knowing subject who reads the word and the world" (Kress, 2020, p. 701).

Finding the Theory: From Critique to Interrogation of Behavior and Discipline Policies

The tradition of critical social science (Crotty, 1998; Giroux, 1983), as explained at the beginning of this chapter ("Critical Moment 1: Being Awakened"), provided evolving theoretical insights and methodologies as a framework in my research journey when I returned to university in the early 1990s. One of the first readings that resonated with me then was the opening chapter in a book by Gibson (1986) titled *Critical theory and education*. Connecting and engaging in dialog in response to this work resulted in many of my tutorial group being awakened and freed to use and understand critical discourse. We became comfortable discussing the real issues and restrictive reforms that we were personally experiencing within our own schools and therefore theorizing them. This gave us more control of our lives. We started to question many of the conventional and restrictive practices, ideas, texts, and ideologies and unravel situations rather than accept them. Gibson (1986) also provided us with the notion that critical theory is not singular—we did not have to confine ourselves to one paradigm because "theory and practice are indivisible" (Gibson, 1986, p. 3). We also began to think about who benefited in our schools and who *did not* because "privileged groups always have an interest in maintaining the status quo to protect their advantages" (Gibson, 1986, p. 3). Venturing on, we began to explore the work of Joe Kincheloe, Peter McLaren, Maxine Greene, Henry Giroux, Michael Apple, Nell Noddings, bell hooks, and of course Paulo Freire. I was also excited to be revisiting the writings of John Dewey and Ivan Illich, who had made big impressions on me during my earlier teacher training in the mid-1970s.

The evolving path of critical social theory (and consequently critical pedagogy) has guided me ever since, along a path to critiquing and resisting neoliberal policy reform such as behavior and discipline policies, not only locally but also globally. I continue to be drawn to the theoretical insights of many influential critical educational theorists in the field to understand the power and oppression that cause "stratification and fragmentation" (Mac an Ghaill & Haywood, 2021); classed injustices and two-tiered schooling (e.g., Gillies & Robinson, 2012; Mills & Pini, 2015; Reay, 2017; Veck & Gunter, 2020); and the dehumanization and marginalization of students in public schools (e.g., Anderson & Oakes, 2014; Smyth & Wrigley, 2013).

Finding the Alternatives: Hope, Agency, and Transformation

Zembylas (2021) encourages researchers and educators like me to continue to cultivate our capacity for critique and, together with a focus on a pedagogy of compassion, become political agents who "create openings to impact youth and society in productive ways" (p. 815). Torres and Van Heertum (2009) agree, explaining that "dialogue and experimentation" produces new knowledge based on *collective lived experience* (p. 230) because "the language of critique unites with the language of possibility" (Aronowitz & Giroux, 1993, p. 46). When as scholars, teachers, and researchers we embrace critical pedagogy as theory and as method, and finally as action, "as an ethical and political practice" (Giroux, 2019, p. 149), consciously stepping out and rejecting the dominant positivist discourses, practices, and injustices such as those outlined throughout this chapter that appear under the banner of behavior and discipline policies, it becomes possible to ask, "how can we do things differently?" (Kress, 2011, p. 262). This activist role is what Freire and Freire (1994) refer to as a "pedagogy of hope"; what Simon (1992) refers to as a "pedagogy of possibility," and what

Greene (1995) expresses as "a release of the imagination." This transformative critical pedagogical role includes:

- *rethinking* and *retheorizing* behavior and discipline polices in education (Furlong, 1991; Millei et al., 2010);
- a search for a vision *that things can be otherwise* (Cassidy & Bates, 2005; Freire, 1998; Halpin, 2003; Kohl, 1998; McInerney, 2004; Smyth, 2011; te Riele, 2010);
- making space for youth to *speak back* (Smyth et al., 2014); and
- imagining a relationally engaging school (Ball, 2016; Bigelow, 2020; Down & Choules, 2017; Fielding & Moss, 2011; Freire, 1970/2005; Meier, 2002; Wright & Kim, 2020).

The Research Context: Critical Policy Ethnography

Ethnography is a powerful tool for detailed, evidence-based critical analysis and social commentary. (Cottle, 2022, p. 331)

As explained in Critical Moment 1, by *being awakened* many of us were fortunate to have the freedom to think about the purpose of our research rather than being preoccupied with method and efficiency—the more instrumental, rational approaches to research which were dominant in the halls of our workplaces and other educational units on offer. This awakening provided us with the knowledge, respectful debate, collaboration, and confidence to explore and enact our individual and collective struggles, all within a critical context. At the same time, we had exposure via our tutorials to a significant collective of Australian critical and feminist educational research scholars from both Deakin and Flinders universities who broadened our knowledge base in critical pedagogy and social justice. These academics included John Smyth, Pat Thomson, Stephen Kemmis, Richard Bates, Jane Kenway, Jill Blackmore, Lawrie Angus, Geoff Shacklock, Lindsay Fitzclarence, Alan Reid, and Robert Hattam. This exposure opened our minds to revolutionary research approaches that enabled us to apply critical social theory into practice. For my own research purposes in my workplace, I found *a home* in blending critical case study and critical ethnography as it suited my purpose of interrogating what was happening to teachers' work within a school effectiveness regime. As Cottle (2022) confirms, it is "vital that the damaging, often hidden consequences of neoliberal restructuring are exposed and challenged" (p. 345).

These research approaches took me on a research journey that provided a critical look inside my own workplace whilst also questioning, observing, and documenting my field. As Cottle explains, I was able to map the "connections between the 'lived experience' of the teachers" and "the broader neoliberal shifts in education policy" (p. 332). I had the privilege of conducting one-on-one, in-depth, semi-structured interviews with 25 of the 70 teachers who worked within my field of practice (Heron High).[1] Further along my research journey, I also found this approach assisted me to interpret and investigate the impact on young people of the Behavior Management in Schools Policy (WA Department of Education, 1998; WA Department of Education and Training, 2001, 2008) and the Student Behavior in Public Schools Policy (WA Department of Education, 2016, 2023). Along this trajectory of policy evolution, I was able to examine in detail the discriminatory practices that were evolving, especially for those young people struggling in disadvantaged schools.

At Anchorage High, I had the opportunity to interview 27 16-year-old secondary students and trace and record firsthand their experiences and interpretations of the school's behavior and discipline policy. After transcribing these interviews, I was able to create a series of narrative portraits which led the way to finding common themes of analysis and discussion that could speak back to policy discourse (see Chapter 5).

Outline of the Book

This introductory chapter concludes with an outline of the structure of the remainder of this book. Chapter 2 serves the purpose of framing the entire book as I elaborate on the broader policy landscape by asking: *What is neoliberalism? And where did it come from?* (Connell, 2013; Connell & Dados, 2014). Chapter 2 also investigates how neoliberalism is reforming education because, as Giroux (2018) argues, neoliberalism impacts on us all globally as "civic subjects" as we are forced into becoming "consuming and marketable subjects" (p. 511). This chapter then focuses specifically on young people, especially the impact and the effects of school policy (Ball, 2006, 2021a, 2021b) and the force of "neoliberal school militat[ing] against their interests" (Smyth, 2020, p. 686). When schools operate like businesses, the focus is on competition, image, "success, merit, rigour and discipline," meaning the untidy students are labeled as deficit, "troublemakers," or "exiled" (Smyth, 2020, pp. 684–685).

The purpose of Chapter 3 is to present the historical context of contemporary behavior and discipline policies by tracing their origins and their evolutions using a genealogical approach based on the writings of various scholars in the field (Foucault, 1975/1979; Giroux, 1983; Millei et al., 2010; Slee, 1988, 1995, 2016; Tait, 2013; Tamboukou, 1999; Taylor et al., 2018). This chapter then traces and focuses on the historical of behavior and discipline policies within Western Australia specifically, identifying major shifts in discourses, when they occurred, why they occurred, and why they happened the way that they did socially, politically, and culturally. This process exposes specific approaches, assumptions, and belief systems. Some of those patterns that continue to linger are then held under both the micro and also wide angled lenses for questioning and urgent critique.

Chapters 4 and 5 trace the historical context by investigating and analyzing behavior and discipline policies in ethnographic detail by getting up close to "map" patterns and evolutions (Tamboukou, 2016, p. 145) as "technicians of power" (Sennett, 2006, p. 158; see also Foucault, 1975/1979). This is achieved by "making the present strange, rather than the past familiar" (Meredyth & Tyler, 1993) and stepping right back *into* the field of two case study secondary schools. Chapter 4 (Heron High), is the case study school in which I was a teacher and apprentice ethnographer between 1995 and 2006 and Chapter 5 (Anchorage High), is the site of the fieldwork for my doctoral dissertation between 2007 and 2009 (Robinson, 2011). The rich data collected in tracing and mapping the ongoing and significant genealogical shifts, patterns, and changing practices in both secondary schools over the 30-year period of the evolution of the Western Australian behavior and discipline policy provides powerful contextual knowledge. As Bright and Smyth (2016), and Beach and Vigo-Arrazola (2021) argue, critical ethnography needs to do more than expose the damage done by neoliberalism in schools; it also needs to focus on transformation and activism. The common themes that emerged from both sites do precisely this as they share the experiences, interpretations, understandings, and perceptions, not only from the author as teacher and ethnographer, and teachers interviewed, but most significantly, in Chapter 5, from the *students themselves*. The passing of time has not diminished the significance of the issues raised by students back then. On the contrary, they remain as relevant and potent today as when I first heard them.

Chapter 6 brings forth these resonating voices directly from the fields to provide invaluable insights and critical knowledge into the present and near future and asks: 'What can be done to rediscover the relational and democratic purposes of education'? To begin answering this question, this chapter begins by invoking the writings of Erich Fromm (1956, 1968), Paulo Freire (1992), Roger Simon (1992), and Maxine Greene (1995) to release social imaginations and seeks robust hope for things to be otherwise and providing the sustenance to "intervene in the world" (Giroux, 2000, p. 139).

Simon's (1992) "horizons of possibility" allows a rethinking, a reimagining, and ultimately a reclaiming of the *public* in *public* education (Gunter, 1997, 2018; Leistyna, 2009; Reid, 2019). This renewed alternative educational narrative requires, first, dismantling the old one, and Monbiot's (2017) metaphor of "climbing out of the wreckage" of neoliberalism serves that purpose. By seeking out new pedagogical directions this chapter continues to struggle to reclaim the relational in education (Riddle & Hickey, 2023; Fielding & Moss, 2011). There are no simple answers or remedies (Smyth, 2020, p. 690) offered here, rather the important questions and perplexities that ultimately lead to a schooling *for* democracy (Riddle, 2022). This is the purpose of the final chapter, and the summarizing framework shares insights of ways and means of young people being engaged in their learning that is respectful and compassionate. This frames what a socially just school within a collaborative learning community can be, offering a sense of hope and possibility for the future.

Note

1 Pseudonyms have been used throughout this book to protect the privacy of all students, teachers, and schools.

References

Anderson, L., & Oakes, J. (2014). The truth about tracking. In P. C. Gorski & K. Zenkov (Eds.), *The big lies of school reform: Finding better solutions for the future of public education* (pp. 199–235). Routledge.

Apple, M. W. (2000). *Official knowledge: Democratic education in a conservative age*. Routledge.

Apple, M. W., Biesta, G., Bright, D., Giroux, H. A., Heffernan, A., McLaren, P., Riddle, S., & Yeatman, A. (2022). Reflections on contemporary challenges and possibilities for democracy and education. *Journal of Educational Administration and History*, 54(3), 245–262. https://doi.org/10.1080/00220620.2022.2052029

Aronowitz, S., & Giroux, H. A. (1993). *Education still under siege*. Bergan & Garvey.

Ayers, W. (2020). I am a revolutionary! In S. Steinberg & B. Down (Eds.), *The Sage handbook of critical pedagogies* (pp. 51–58). Sage.

Ball, S. J. (2006). *Education policy and social class: The selected works of Stephen J. Ball*. Routledge.

Ball, S. J. (2016). Neoliberal education? Confronting the slouching beast. *Policy Futures in Education, 14*(8), 1046–1059.

Ball, S. J (2021a). *The education debate* (4th ed.). Policy Press.

Ball, S. J. (2021b). Response: Policy? Policy research? How absurd? *Critical Studies in Education, 62*(3), 387–393.

Beach, D., & Vigo-Arrazola, M. (2021). Critical ethnographies of education and for social and educational transformation: A meta-ethnography. *Qualitative Inquiry, 27*(6), 677–688.

Biesta, G., Wainwright, E., & Aldridge, D. (2022). Editorial: A case for diversity in educational research and educational practice. *British Educational Research Journal, 48*(1), 1–4.

Bigelow, B. (2020). We need to ask our students to dream—And to dream big. *Rethinking Schools, 34*(3). https://rethinkingschools.org/articles/we-need-to-ask-our-students-to-dream-and-to-dream-big.

Bright, G., & Smyth, J. (2016). Editors' introduction. *Ethnography and Education, 11*(2), 123–128.

Cassidy, W., & Bates, A. (2005). "Drop-outs" and "push-outs": Finding hope at a school that actualizes the ethic of care. *American Journal of Education, 112*(1), 66–102.

Connell, R. (2013). The neoliberal cascade and education: An essay on the market agenda and its consequences. *Critical Studies in Education, 54*(2), 99–112.

Connell, R., & Dados, N. (2014). Where in the world does neoliberalism come from? The market agenda in southern perspective. *Theory & Society, 43*(2), 117–138.

Cottle, M. (2022). What can Bourdieu offer the ethnographer in neoliberal times: Reflecting on methodological possibilities. *Ethnography and Education, 17*(4), 331–347.

Crotty, M. (1998). *The foundations of social research*. Allen & Unwin.

Down, B., & Choules, K. (2017). Towards a pedagogy of personalisation: What can we learn from students? *Curriculum Perspectives, 37*, 135–145.

Fielding, M., & Moss, P. (2011). *Radical education and the common school: A democratic alternative*. Routledge.

Foucault, M. (1979). *Discipline and punish: The birth of the prison* (A. Sheridan, Trans.). Peregrine. (Original work published 1975).

Freire, P. (1992). Foreword (D. Macedo, Trans.). In P. Leonard & P. McLaren (Eds.), *Paulo Freire: A critical encounter* (pp. ix–xii). Routledge.

Freire, P. (1998). *Pedagogy of freedom: Ethics, democracy, and civic courage*. Rowman & Littlefield.

Freire, P. (2004). *Pedagogy of indignation*. Paradigm Publishers.

Freire, P. (2005). *Pedagogy of the oppressed* (M. B. Ramos, Trans.). Continuum. (Original work published 1970).

Freire, P., & Freire, A. (1994). *Pedagogy of hope: Reliving Pedagogy of the oppressed*. Continuum.

Fromm, E. (1956). *The art of loving*. Open Road Integrated Media.

Fromm, E. (1968). *The revolution of hope: Toward a humanized technology*. Bantam Books.

Furlong, V. J. (1991). Disaffected pupils: Reconstructing the sociological perspective. *British Journal of Sociology of Education, 12*(3), 293–307.

Gibson, R. (1986). *Critical theory and education*. Hodder & Stoughton.

Gillies, V., & Robinson, Y. (2012). "Including" while excluding: Race, class and behaviour support units. *Race Ethnicity and Education, 15*(2), 157–174.

Giroux, H. A. (1983). *Theory and resistance in education: A pedagogy for the opposition.* Bergin & Garvey.

Giroux, H. A. (2000). *Stealing innocence: Corporate culture's war on children.* Palgrave.

Giroux, H. A. (2012). *Education and the crisis of public values: Challenging the assault on teachers, students, and public education.* Peter Lang.

Giroux, H. A. (2018). When schools become dead zones of the imagination: A critical pedagogy manifesto. In K. J. Saltman & A. J. Means (Eds.), *The Wiley handbook of global educational reform* (pp. 503–516). John Wiley & Sons.

Giroux, H. A. (2019). Toward a pedagogy of educated hope under casino capitalism. *Pedagogía y Saberes, 50,* 147–151.

Green, S., & Siegel, B. (Directors). (2002). *The weather underground* [Film]. Free History Project. https://www.imdb.com/title/tt0343168/

Greene, M. (1995). *Releasing the imagination: Essays on education, the arts, and social change.* Jossey-Bass.

Gunter, H. (1997). *Rethinking education: The consequences of Jurassic management.* Cassell.

Gunter, H. (2009). The "C" word in educational research: An appreciative response. *Critical Studies in Education, 50*(1), 93–102.

Gunter, H. (2018). *The politics of public education.* Policy Press.

Halpin, D. (2003). *Hope and education: The role of the utopian imagination.* RoutledgeFalmer.

Kenway, J. (2011). A melancholic melody. In R. Tinning & K. Sirna (Eds.), *Education, social justice and the legacy of Deakin University: Reflections of the Deakin diaspora* (pp. 93–103). Sense Publishers.

Kenway, J., & Fahey, J. (2009). *Globalizing the research imagination.* Routledge.

Kohl, H. (1998). *The discipline of hope: Learning from a lifetime of teaching.* New Press.

Kress, T. M. (2011). Inside the "thick wrapper" of critical pedagogy and research. *International Journal of Qualitative Studies in Education, 24*(3), 261–266.

Kress, T. M. (2020). Critical pedagogy as research. In S. Steinberg & B. Down (Eds.), *The Sage handbook of critical pedagogies* (Vol. 2, pp. 694–703). Sage.

Leistyna, P. (2009). Preparing for public life: Education, critical theory, and social justice. In W. Ayers, T. Quinn, & D. Stovall (Eds.), *The handbook of social justice in education* (pp. 51–58). Rowman & Littlefield.

Mac an Ghaill, M., & Haywood, C. (2021). Ethnography, methodological autonomy, and self-representational space: A reflexive millennial generation of Muslim young men. *Ethnography and Education, 16*(4), 457–474.

McInerney, P. (2004). *Making hope practical: School reform for social justice.* Post Pressed.

Meier, D. (2002). *In schools we trust: Creating communities of learning in an era of testing and standardization.* Beacon Press.

Meredyth, D., & Tyler, D. (1993). Introduction. In D. Meredyth & D. Tyler (Eds.), *Child and citizen: Genealogies of schooling and subjectivity* (pp. 1–10). Institute for Cultural Studies, Griffin University.

Millei, Z., Griffiths, T. G., & Parkes R. J. (Eds.). (2010). *Re-theorizing discipline in education: Problems, politics & possibilities.* Peter Lang.

Mills, M., & Pini, B. (2015). Punishing kids: The rise of the "boot camp." *International Journal of Inclusive Education, 19*(3), 270–284.

Monbiot, G. (2017). *Out of the wreckage: A new politics for an age of crisis.* Verso.

Reay, D. (2017). *Miseducation: Inequality, education and the working classes.* Policy Press.

Reid, A. (2019). *Changing Australian education: How policy is taking us backwards and what can be done about it.* Allen & Unwin.

Riddle, S. (2022). *Schooling for democracy: Towards a more caring, inclusive and sustainable future.* Routledge.

Riddle, S., & Hickey, A. (2023). Reclaiming relationality in education policy: Towards a more authentic relational pedagogy. *Critical Studies in Education, 64*(3), 267–282. https://doi.org/10.1080/17508487.2022.2132414

Robinson, J. (2011). *"Troubling" behaviour management: listening to student voice* [Ph.D. thesis]. Murdoch University.

Robinson, K. (2013, May 10). *How to escape education's death valley* [Video]. YouTube. https://www.youtube.com/watch?v=wX78iKhInsc

Sennett, R. (2006). *The culture of the new capitalism.* Yale University Press.

Shor, I. (1992). *Empowering education: Critical teaching for social change.* University of Chicago Press.

Simon, R. (1992). *Teaching against the grain: Texts for a pedagogy of possibility.* Bergin & Garvey.

Slee, R. (1988). Policy development: Discipline or control? In R. Slee (Ed.), *Discipline and schools: A curriculum perspective* (pp. 2–28). Macmillan.

Slee, R. (1995). *Changing theories and practices of discipline.* Falmer Press.

Slee, R. (2016). Goodbye Mr Chips, hello Dr Phil? In A. Sullivan, B. Johnson, & B. Lucas (Eds.), *Challenging dominant views on student behaviour at school: Answering back* (pp. 63–76). Springer.

Smyth, J. (2011). *Critical pedagogy for social justice.* Continuum International Publishing Group.

Smyth, J. (2020). A critical pedagogy of working-class schooling: A call to activist theory and practice. In S. Steinberg & B. Down (Eds.), *The Sage handbook of critical pedagogies* (pp. 681–693). Sage.

Smyth, J., Down, B., & McInerney, P. (2014). *The socially just school: Making space for youth to speak back.* Springer.

Smyth, J., & Hattam. R. (2002). Early school leaving and the cultural geography of high schools. *British Educational Research Journal, 28*(3), 375–397.

Smyth, J., & Wrigley, T. (2013). *Living on the edge: Rethinking poverty, class and schooling.* Peter Lang.

Steinberg, S. (2010). Preface. In Z. Millei, T. G. Griffiths, & R. J. Parkes (Eds.), *Re-theorizing discipline in education: Problems, politics & possibilities* (pp. i–xii). Peter Lang.

Steinberg, S., & Down, B. (Eds.). (2020). *The Sage handbook of critical pedagogies* (Vol. 1–3). Sage.

Tait, G. (2013). *Making sense of mass education.* Cambridge University Press.

Tamboukou, M. (1999). Writing genealogies: An exploration of Foucault's strategies for doing research. *Discourse: Studies in the Cultural Politics of Education, 20*(2), 201–217.

Tamboukou, M. (2016). Education as action/the adventure of education: Thinking with Arendt and Whitehead. *Journal of Educational Administration and History, 48*(2), 136–147.

Taylor, E., Deakin, J., & Kupchik, A. (2018). The changing landscape of school discipline, surveillance, and social control. In J. Deakin, E. Taylor, & A. Kupchik (Eds.), *The Palgrave international handbook of school discipline, surveillance, and social control* (pp. 1–12). Palgrave.

te Riele, K. (2010). Philosophy of hope: Concepts and applications for working with marginalized youth. *Journal of Youth Studies, 13*(1), 35–46.

Torres, C. A., & van Heertum, R. (2009). Education and domination. In G. Sykes, B. Schneider, & D. N. Plank (Eds.), *Handbook of education policy research* (pp. 221–239). Routledge.

Veck, W., & Gunter, H. (2020). *Hannah Arendt on educational thinking and practice in dark times: Education for a world crisis*. Bloomsbury Academic.

WA Department of Education. (1998). *Behaviour Management in Schools Policy*.

WA Department of Education. (2016). *Student Behaviour in Public Schools Policy*. Government of Western Australia.

WA Department of Education. (2023). *Student Behaviour in Public Schools Policy*. Government of Western Australia.

WA Department of Education and Training. (2001). *Behaviour Management in Schools*.

WA Department of Education and Training. (2008). Behaviour Management in Schools. http://policies.det.wa.edu.au/our_policies/

Wright, J. S., & Kim, T. (2020). Reframing community (dis)engagement: The discursive connection between undemocratic policy enactment, minoritized communities and resistance. *Journal of Education Policy, 37*(2), 1–19. https://doi.org/10.1080/02680939.2020.1777467

Zembylas, M. (2021). Adorno on democratic pedagogy and the education of emotions: Pedagogical insights for resisting right-wing extremism. *Policy Futures in Education, 19*(7), 809–825.

· 2 ·

THE BROADER EDUCATIONAL POLICY LANDSCAPE

Introduction

Paulo Freire (2004) explains that "freedom" is not a given gift but "earned by those who enrich themselves through the struggle" (p. 120). Maverick Zhang (2022) experienced many struggles related to the impact of neoliberalism on his cultural upbringing, scholarship, and emotional wellbeing. In the intricate network of his writing, he connects these experiences to a critique of neoliberalism, which is an act of resistance and enrichment for him. Even though Zhang is half my age, his experiences of "being awakened" align with many of those I shared throughout the first chapter of this book. Zhang, however, in contrast to my outback country town upbringing in Western Australia in the late 1950s, was born and raised in China during the one child policy of the early 1990s.

Zhang's story reveals a capacity to reflect on, step outside of, and be critical of the everyday influences of neoliberalism on his life trajectory and the personal decisions that he was forced to make about where to go and what to do—and hence what pathways to take. After losing his brother/cousin to suicide, as with many of his compatriots, due to enormous pressures to compete academically and fulfill his family's dreams of entering college, Zhang's compassion for humanity and an uprising of hope and transformation are powerful messages. Like the American sociologist C. W. Mills (1959/1971), Zhang endeavors to shift the focus from the "personal troubles" of his family and community to "public issues of social structure" (2022, p. 14): "it was not my dad. It was the neoliberal push for competition and economical, the institutionalized subject positions, and assumptions associated by my sociolinguistic identities that I have long been struggling with" (p. 18).

Freire (1970/2005) refers to the "awakening" revealed in Zhang's story as "conscientizagdo" (translated as conscientization), "a deepening of the attitude of awareness characteristic of all emergence" (p. 109). The purpose of this chapter is to bring this awakening and awareness to the public issue of school discipline. Like Zhang, I endeavor to locate the "personal troubles" of school discipline in the broader context of neoliberalism. In pursuing this task, I draw on Burawoy's (2009) observation that "everyone is a theorist in the sense that some coherent account of the world is necessary to live in community with others" (p. 269).

In this chapter, I discuss the nature and origins of neoliberalism and its implications for education, specifically school discipline. I am interested in tracing how neoliberalism has infected education systems around the globe that act like a virus, or what Sahlberg (2021, p. 173) names the Global Education Reform Movement. I then move on to examine the effect of this reform in the Australian context and describe Smyth's (2020, pp. 686–687) dispositions of a neoliberal school. The implications for and interventions into school policy and practice are then discussed, firstly by examining the influence of international organizations such as the OECD, and secondly by tracing the cascade of neoliberal reform as it unfolds more specifically at the school level. Central to my argument here is the way in which neoliberalism has eroded the democratic purposes of education through the escalating use of deficit ideology, zero tolerance, and eventually exclusion from schooling. Finally, I describe and advocate a more democratic and humane approach to education founded on the socially just and the relational dimension of teaching and learning, a place in which young people can flourish. But first I want to say something about my own evolving criticality and what is happening to education, particularly in connection to the issue of school discipline.

My Evolving Criticality

I begin by referring to several key scholars who have influenced my own thinking. I was initially attracted to Kincheloe's (2007) argument that an evolving criticality "is uninterested in any theory—no matter how fashionable—that does not directly address the needs of victims of oppression and the suffering they must endure" (p. 19). In a similar vein, Smyth (2011), a remarkable Australian critical scholar, encapsulates the role of theory in the following way: "theory is inextricably embedded in the practice and the experience of everyday lives, and how practice, experience and everyday lives are reshaped and reinformed by theory" (p. 145).

Both Kincheloe and Smyth, in their own way, point to the relevance of theory in addressing the needs of the most vulnerable and powerless by puncturing the myths of objective knowledge and everyday practices. This is not a method per se but a moral and political commitment to change the world for the better (Giroux, 2019, p. 149). Leistyna (2007) explains that an evolving criticality or "developing critical consciousness" does not mean insisting that we must think in a certain way but rather "to think more deeply about the issues and relations of power" (p. 117). In my case, this involves a critique of school discipline in the context of neoliberalism and the ways in which it contributes to and sustains unequal power relations.

Knight (1991) warned us over three decades ago that education policy and school programs needed to be "informed by a principled theory of educational purpose [. . . because] without sound theory as a guide, there is the risk that school discipline policy could be full of dubious psychology or strengthened notions of mindless authoritarianism" (p. 119). Educational reforms that treat schools and students as "civic subjects" who are "consuming and marketable beings" (Giroux, 2018, p. 511) must be reckoned with, for example, the OECD's (2023) call for school improvement based on more efficient and effective "classroom management and student behaviour management" (p. 24). International agencies such as the OCED are neither neutral nor innocent bystanders as education policies are reshaped under the guise of neoliberalism. For them, the purpose of education is measured largely in terms of economic growth and human capital formation.

In countering these tendencies, Nikolakaki (2012) believes that critical pedagogy is "one of the few radical transformative pedagogies [. . .] that has a historic role to play [. . .] to break the culture of silence, to demystify the social imaginary [. . .] and to promote humanization again" (p. 16). Nikolakaki (2012) shares some alarming statistics about the devastating impact of neoliberalism on humanity during the 21st century:

- Nearly a billion people are unable to read a book or sign their names.
- One billion children live in poverty.
- 640 million live without proper shelter.
- 400 million have no access to safe water.
- 270 million have no access to health services.
- In 2003, 10.6 million died before they reached the age of five (p. 16).

Kress (2011) argues that once we scholars and practitioners get *inside* the thick wrapper of critical pedagogy and unwrap a place and position to share our common goals of a more humanizing education, we can then ask, "How can we do things differently?" (p. 262). Ultimately, that is the purpose of this book.

What Is Neoliberalism and Where Did It Come From?

> It is familiar that indices of economic inequality tend to rise under neoliberal rule.
> (Connell & Dados, 2014, p. 133)

Connell (2013) describes neoliberalism as "the latest mutation in a sprawling world-wide regime, which forged a new settlement between military, political and business elites in the global periphery, and their counterparts in the metropole" (p. 101). The complex work of Connell and Dados (2014) provides a Southern perspective on neoliberalism, in contrast to the many interpretations prioritized historically in the global North where there has been a shift in ideology making the theories of where it came from and what it is insufficient in a critical sense. The authors argue that "neoliberalism is not a projection of Northern ideology or policy, but a re-weaving of worldwide economic and social relationships" (p. 124). Without wanting to oversimplify the authors' sophisticated arguments, I take some liberty here to summarize their main points.

Connell and Dados (2014) begin with the central theme of the market's role in development strategies across the global South including deregulation (economic rationalism) to avoid the collapse of privileged living standards for the North. The authors then outline the interlacing of global trade across the South with political coercion and the formative role of the state, including the military. An escalating and heterogeneous global capitalism and the expansion of world commodity trade has resulted in the expansion of land and agriculture, minerals, informal economics, the transformation of rural societies, and the growth of mega-cities, all of which took its toll and has "stakes in political struggle" (Connell & Dados, 2014, p. 132).

Education viewed as a product is a pivotal ingredient in this worldwide market logic via "international league tables for schools, corporatization of universities, restructuring of teaching workforces, and the redefinition of education systems as export industries pursuing comparative advantage" (Connell & Dados, 2014, p. 132), all of which are "wreaking havoc" (Nikolakaki, 2012, p. 27) on the lives of young people. The problem, according to Giroux and Paul (2022), is that "under neoliberalism, all problems are personal and individual, making it almost impossible to translate private troubles into wider systemic considerations." As a result, schools "remain caught in the vice-like grip of the greatest untested social and political experiment ever attempted in human history" (Smyth, 2019a, p. 25).

Neoliberal Global School Reform

> It is important to realize that education is a part of society. It is not something alien, something that stands outside. (Apple, 2015, p. 305)

In this section I examine broader economic and political forces that continue to shape education. My concern is the way the forces of neoliberalism function to erode the capacity for democratic schooling and contribute to the corrosion of relationships within education. When a neoliberal regime drives the momentum of public policy, that is, "the private inserts itself" (Ball, 2006, p. 135) through economic rationalism, then public places and spaces, including schools, are not only commodified but also blamed for global economic and social woes. Policy protocols and practices are not typically questioned nor debated in this system and yet continue to be legitimized through the marketplace metaphor, with students "concomitantly" (Ball, 2006, p. 135) treated as human capital (Apple, 1999, p. 9).

An example of the marketplace metaphor is evident in the World Economic Forum's (2020) *Schools of the future* white paper, which claims that "the private sector can play a key role in fostering the right kind of problem-solving to help children transition to the future of work" (p. 13). Rizvi et al. (2022) argue, however, that this promise to students of stable employment and opportunities is negligent, as "the conditions of work have become ever more uncertain and precarious" (p. 9).

Sahlberg (2021, p. 178) provides another example with "school choice" as a global product, in which a "voucher system" introduced in Chile in the 1980s was followed in the 1990s by Sweden, and continued to spread as "charter schools" throughout the United States in the 2000s, and then as "secondary academics" in England in the 2010s. The ideology of school choice also led to an increase in private and independent schools throughout Australia (Sahlberg, 2021, p. 178) and New Zealand (McDonald et al., 2023, p. 308). Reay (2022) describes the likely fallout of this global system of choice in England's proposal (set out in the Education White Paper, DfE, 2022) to move all schools to academy status by 2030, "effectively bringing the state school system to an end" (Reay, 2022, p. 430).

Neoliberalism in Australia

In a convincing and carefully crafted essay on the market agenda and its consequences, Connell (2013) argues that the reach of the market became even wider in Australia under the neoliberal cascade:

> Many public assets have been privatized—in Australia including the national airline, the national bank and the national telecommunications system. Neoliberals have had astonishing success in creating markets for things whose commodification was once almost unimaginable: drinking water, body parts and social welfare among them. Welfare is commodified by putting the provision of services up for tender and forcing the public agencies that formerly provided them to compete with NGOs, churches and companies to win the tenders. (p. 100)

Welch (2007) agrees that Australia in particular "licensed considerable privatisation of services in education" (p. 6). Welch (2007) also explains that this occurred because Australia as a nation-state reduced its responsibility for funding public services under economic rationalism, whilst at the same time increasing regulation under the name of accountability to circumvent the nation-state's risk of failure (p. 6). Smyth and McInerney (2007) elaborate that, as governments at both state and federal levels within Australia sculpted the educational landscape, so too were public policies implemented and shaped by the "privatiz[ation] of utilities and a user pays approach" (p. 53). In this manner, international competitiveness connected the institutional practice of schooling directly to the marketplace (Knight, 1997, p. 82), then ultimately it was "the market" that continued to control government public schooling in Australia including the "Australian Curriculum," "Professional Standards for

Teachers," "Safe Schools Framework," and expanding national testing regimes (Johnson & Sullivan, 2016, p. 34).

Even though Western Australia, the state in which I live and where I have worked throughout my lifetime as a teacher and researcher, has constitutional responsibility for public education as a residual power, the transfer of sole authority over income collection to the Commonwealth government during World War 2 (using section 96 of the constitution), paved the way for federal influence and intervention. This change occurred partly following the collapse of the post-war boom experienced by all OECD nations, forcing the public sector, including the education system I was schooled in and continued to work in, to become more efficient. This in turn forced state departments such as the Western Australian Education Department to have less say in detailed policy as it was replaced by a broad-based "one-size-fits-all" model. What this meant for Western Australian schools was greater responsibility for the adaptation and implementation of directions determined from the center (Lingard et al., 1995, p. 82) as the "neoliberal cascade" (Connell, 2013) continued to descend.

The Neoliberal School

> What goes on in the classroom today has long and complex tentacles that reach into the open social systems that students inhabit, and trying to deal with behaviour issues in a hermetically sealed way is an exercise doomed to certain failure. (Smyth, 2011, pp. 10–11)

This subsection steps inside classrooms to glimpse how they may be experienced as they are "radically recast" into a "neoliberal school" (Smyth, 2020, p. 689), relying heavily on keeping young people "managed and under control" (Ladson-Billings, 2014, p. 11). Smyth (2020) lists thirteen dispositions of a neoliberal school. I have taken the liberty of summarizing them here to highlight just how alien and discriminatory middle-class compulsory schooling has become for many young people, especially those "living in neighbourhoods of poverty" (Smyth & Wrigley, 2013, p. 196) who are not in a place nor position to compete:

1. The primary focus is upon *the unit of the individual* and individualism.
2. *Competition* is the source of all individual and institutional inspiration and improvement.
3. *Delayed gratification* is crucial in the production of meritocratic rewards in the future.

4. *Failure* follows from lack of effort, application, and individual dysfunction—it is deserved.
5. *Privatization of the self* is the way out of the mediocrity of the collective and the way to foster innovation.
6. There is no such thing as an *unlevel playing field*—only opportunities forgone or lack of aspiration.
7. The engine for sorting out educational worth and value resides in the *exercise of choice*.
8. Education has to be *future focused* rather than becoming mired in immediacy or acquiescing to emotionality. (We must act objectively and rationally.)
9. *Stratification is a desirable*, crucial, and inevitable outcome of the differential application of effort. (This includes rankings and hierarchies.)
10. Educational context is *unimportant*—place is a neutral concept of no educational significance. (Neoliberalism is skeptical of social forces.)
11. The way to deal with *difference in ability* is to sort individuals into tracks or trajectories best suited to innate ability—hence the importance of calibration and measurement.
12. Students are *"fitted into place"* in a hierarchy.
13. *Heroic* leaders are those who avail themselves to be autonomous and unleash the unbridled potential of everyone in the neoliberal school (Smyth, 2020, pp. 686–687).

Implications of the "Neoliberal School" for School Discipline

Considering these recast dispositions of a neoliberal school, this section focuses on implications relating specifically to school discipline policies; firstly, by discussing the influence and interventions of international organizations (especially the OECD) into school discipline and, secondly, by explaining how the cascade of neoliberal reform unfolds at the school level.

OECD and School Discipline

The OECD and other international organizations, which are "unelected and unaccountable" (Smyth et al., 2014, p. 17), with a "powerful steering role in prioritising the economic over the social" (Reay, 2022, p. 425), promise "significant gains in [. . .] national economies" (Sahlberg, 2021, p. 126). Such promises are especially pertinent if countries score well in programs such as the Programme for International Student Assessment (PISA), accelerating the shift to rigid and prescribed curriculum, including the "National Curriculum" in England, the "New National Education Standards" in Germany, the "Common Core State Standards" in the United States, and the "Australian Curriculum" (Sahlberg, 2021, p. 179).

In 2006, when Fazal Rizvi and Bob Lingard wrote about the changing nature of the OECD's educational work, they expressed curiosity and concern, because it had "always been linked to the broad economic purposes of the organization" (Rizvi & Lingard, 2006, p. 259). The latest OECD (2023) report on education in Australia confirms that what continues to be measured is performance on tests such as PISA, "exacerbat[ing] inequalities within and between nations" (Rizvi & Lingard, 2006, p. 260).

The OECD (2023) report *Education policy outlook in Australia* collated survey information on the "disciplinary climate in schools" and concluded that "Australia was among the least favourable [...] with an index of -0.2 (OECD average: 0.04)" (p. 23), making "Australian classrooms amongst the world's most disorderly" (Senate, Education and Employment References Committee, 2024, p. 1). What was especially concerning is, in response to an ostensibly innocent measurement "index" by the OECD, an Australian Senate committee recommended a "behaviour curriculum" survey (Rec. 7), possibly to be completed in the next PISA testing (Senate, Education and Employment References Committee, 2023, p. 58). This report also suggested that the Australian Curriculum, Assessment and Reporting Authority should "strengthen the focus on behavior within the Australian Curriculum by specifically introducing a 'Behaviour Curriculum'" (p. ix).

In the final report on *The issue of increasing disruption in Australian school classrooms* (Senate, Education and Employment References Committee, 2024), only one recommendation remained from the original seven in the interim report. This recommendation was that "the Senate refer an inquiry into declining academic standards in Australian schools" (Rec. 1.28, p. 9). The focus on academic performance and "standardization" in the global market, connected and linked to student behavior and conduct in classrooms could not be more blatant! Slee (2011) argues, as Rizvi and Lingard (2006, p. 260) also warned, that the global power of organizations such as the OECD "should not be underestimated" (Slee, 2011, p. 159). That is because these organizations continue to "exert a gravity that draws jurisdictions in disparate countries to converge around invented measures of performance and values" (Slee, 2011,

p. 159). Australian schools in this Commonwealth report, for example, are compared with those countries ranking the highest in "disciplinary indexes" (Japan, Korea, Austria); in academic performance in mathematics and sciences (Singapore, China, Japan); and in literacy (Singapore, Ireland, Japan) (Senate, Education and Employment References Committee, 2024, p. 4). The authors of this report also advised:

> that Australia should examine how high performing countries are achieving better results than Australia, including the extent to which the experience of these countries can inform Australian schools, and how funding for students in Australia and other countries correlates with student performance and academic standards. (p. 9)

When international organizations such as the OECD "enter the same field of children's well-being" (Fielding & Moss, 2011, p. 20) they become predominantly organized and managed to "operate in ways that sustain, maintain and enhance their positional image in the education marketplace" (Smyth, 2020, p. 685).

The Cascade of Neoliberal Reform Unfolds

As the cascade of neoliberal reform unfolds at the school level, those students already "living on the edge" (Smyth & Wrigley, 2013) are those most directly impacted. Nowhere is this more apparent than the enactment of behavior and management policies espoused by the proponents of zero tolerance or "get tough" approaches. Smyth (2020) explains what happens as neoliberalism infiltrates school behavior and discipline policy:

> Students who present as troublesome, disruptive, disengaged, recalcitrant, or who distinguish themselves by "speaking back" to what they regard as the irrelevance of the curriculum or the stupidification of the pedagogy of the school, are positioned "outside" of, or exiled from, school literally and metaphorically. (pp. 684–685)

The many regulatory "panopticon" (Foucault, 1975/1979) approaches enacted in neoliberal schools position students *outside* of school by situating them *inside* detention centers (now ironically labeled inclusion centers) and stigmatize them as "at risk". These students, their emotions, and identities are often regulated to conform and comply to school structures and cultures that do not accommodate their needs through an "ethos of competitive individualism in the shape of testing" and "sponsoring residual tracks for the growing second-and third-tier students" (Slee, 2011, p. 143). This is not inclusive education.

In the remainder of this section, I continue this discussion on how neoliberalism is enacted at the level of school discipline policy and practice under three headings: (i) deficit ideology (at risk, individualizing, pathologizing), (ii) zero tolerance (get tough), and (iii) exclusion (detention, behavior centers, boot camps).

Deficit Ideology

Gorski (2014) explains what is meant by deficit ideology:

> A set of beliefs (or ideology) that pegs people in poverty as morally, intellectually, and even spiritually deficient. Equally sinister, it attributes outcome inequalities, such as those related to high school graduation rates or standardized test scores, to that deficiency. In fact, the deficit ideologue generally believes that poverty itself is an outcome of an individual's deficiencies. Everybody has an equal opportunity to succeed, the thinking goes, if people just work hard enough. (p. 129)

It is the poor, therefore, and working-class youth and their families who are too often blamed and their schools made accountable. Gorski (2014) goes on to argue that the notions of "inclusive" education, meritocracy, and educational equality are myths:

> Most often neoliberal education reformers who sell deficit ideology along with their corporate-friendly reforms have, during the most recent wave of school reform, pointed the blaming finger at low-income parents for not being involved enough in their children's education, at teachers and administrators in high-poverty schools for not adequately boosting students' test scores, at teachers' unions, and at just about everybody and everything other than the underlying cause of outcome inequalities: poverty itself. (p. 130)

In 1996, the Students at Risk program was implemented in Australia as a Commonwealth policy to identify students who needed support because they were considered most at risk of not completing secondary school. The Australian Law Reform Commission (1997) supported further implementation of this program as "a means of ensuring that all children are better educated, more employable and less likely to turn to crime out of necessity or boredom," while adding that "teachers require appropriate professional development training in identifying students at risk" (para. 10.26, Rec. 39). As Gillies (2016) argues, what is happening under neoliberalism, as young people are identified as "at risk," is that "disadvantage becomes envisaged as a psychological barrier to learning through a conflation of poverty with personal deficit" (p. 75).

Another example of neoliberal deficit ideology appears in a national research project: the Australian Child and Adolescent Survey on Mental Health and Wellbeing, reported by Lawrence et al. (2016). Key findings from this research included that one in seven Australian children aged 4–17 years had met diagnostic criteria for a mental disorder over that year. This research was followed by an investigation into the impact of mental disorders on attendance at school (Lawrence et al., 2019). The researchers concluded that, during "the secondary school years, anxiety disorders, major depressive disorder and conduct disorder are all associated with similarly high levels of absenteeism" (p. 11). The proposed solution was "early identification and appropriate management of mental disorders [which] may also help to improve general school attendance" (p. 18).

Slee (2011) argues that what emerges in this kind of research are set "parameters for knowledge and discourse" (p. 136), hence, "particular patterns of inclusion and exclusion" (p. 136). Both studies by Lawrence et al. (2016, 2019) were funded by Australian Government departments (Health and Education), and further research of this kind continues via the Telethon Kids Institute (see, e.g., Hancock et al., 2021). As fear coalesces around mental health and disengagement with schooling, young people become framed as "'bundles of pathologies' that have to be remedied or 'fixed'" (Down, 2016, p. 90), and in turn are perceived as "maladjusted," "troubled," "disruptive," "disorderly," "uncontrollable," "dangerous," and "genetically compromised" (Gillies, 2011, p. 187; Slee, 2011, p. 149). In short, they are "unwanted incursions into the smooth running of the school" (Harwood, 2006, p. 5).

Zero Tolerance Policies

> Students in schools are not sealed off from the "external [social] toxins" when they come into schools and classrooms. (Smyth, 2011, p. 11)

Ayers et al. (2001) reported that, due to the rise of zero tolerance policies in the city of Chicago, 90 children, overwhelmingly African American and Latino, were being suspended or expelled from their public schools each week, the majority for nonviolent misdeeds. These schools were being turned into fortresses with "electronic searches, locked doors, armed police, surveillance cameras, patrolled cafeterias, and weighty rule books defining the landscape" (p. xiii). Zero tolerance policies had created "a downward spiral of further punishment and greater social alienation" (p. xv). Clarke et al. (2021) also reported on the growth of authoritarian and punitive behavior policies and practices in English schools that undermined democratic purposes of education, "with catch-cry labels such as 'no excuses' and 'zero tolerance'" (p. 188), converting schools "to becoming white, middle class and able-bodied" (p. 197). Reay (2017) reported from her research, also in England, that zero tolerance "operates as an enormous academic sieve, sorting out the educational winners from the losers" (p. 26), with ethnic minority groups labeled as "monkeys" and the predominantly white, middle-class top group labeled as "cheetahs" (p. 25). In summary, zero tolerance policies "create communities in which youth and adults who most need help cannot safely come forwards [. . .] because their problems remain silenced underground" (Fine & Smith, 2001, p. 258).

Exclusion

Gillies (2016) argues that the deficit model together with zero tolerance policies as outlined above have driven the escalation in the number of "behavior centers" and "referral units" throughout the globe. These separate hubs often fail to connect with the real lives of the young people who must attend them because they are often focused on psychological and mental health factors and overlook everyday realities (Gillies, 2016, p. 182). Mills and Pini (2015) also report on the rise of boot camps and their providers in Australia, and in England, and argue that they "work to construct young people as an escalating and uncontrollable problem" (p. 271), masking the impact of other educational and societal structures such as the inflexible school curricula and pedagogies that marginalized and alienated them in the first place. In addition, the authors argue that the "militaristic logic underpinning these camps" (Mills & Pini, 2015, p. 280) exacerbates the problems many of these young people have already experienced including emotional and physical abuse and trauma, "ensuring many fell further behind their classmates" (Gillies, 2016, p. 182).

Instead, a Place to Flourish

> Schools need to be places where students can flourish free from intimidation, fear, anxiety, threats and retribution. (Down, 2016, p. 88)

Connell and Dados (2014) explain that, to really understand the impact of neoliberalism worldwide, we need to look at its roots, "from below," and the policies and practices that have emerged from marketization, and "address large-scale social and cultural changes" (p. 134). According to Aronowitz and Giroux (1993), this requires uniting the "language of critique" with the "language of possibility" to navigate "the conditions necessary for new forms of culture, alternative social practices, new modes of communication, and a practical vision for the future" (p. 46).

Down (2016) argues that to be "truly serious about addressing the persistent and protracted problem of mis/behaviour in schools [...] will require a major paradigm shift of thought and action" (p. 89). One approach, for example, could be "to treat young people and the backgrounds they come from as being 'at promise' and as having strengths of one kind or another" (p. 90). Earlier in this chapter, I borrowed Smyth's (2020) thirteen identifying dispositions of the "neoliberal school" as a form of critique. As a counterpoint, Fine and Smith (2001) have recommended features of schools that would make them more equitable, educational, and safe places for all. I have once again paraphrased these authors' suggestions:

- They are small and encourage community engagement and public accountability.
- They are places of trust and respect between youth and adults and among youth.
- They are sites in "which learning is organized as an opportunity to explore, challenge, revise, and critique the world *as it is*, and to create a world *not yet*." (p. 261). Youth imagination is not censored.
- They work *with* communities to build trust, social capital, and long-term sustainable opportunities for support (Fine & Smith, 2001, pp. 260–261).

Down and Choules (2017) agree that if we want to genuinely engage students then they need to have more say, ownership, and control over "who, what and from whom they learn," and once "these conditions are brought into existence, we see evidence of enhanced relationships with peers, teachers, families, communities and other significant adults" (p. 135).

Conclusion

In a culture in which the marketing orientation prevails, and in which material success is the outstanding value, there is little reason to be surprised that human love relations follow the same pattern of exchange which governs the commodity and the labor market. (Fromm, 1956, p. 4)

As the private sector expands in global influence and takes greater control of policy and process from the public sector, there are many human costs.

Neoliberalism has become so pervasive "that to think otherwise, is to be like a fish out of water, or worse, to be engaged in heresy or treason" (Smyth, 2019b, p. 469). Throughout this chapter, I have used an evolving critical lens to explain neoliberalism, where it came from, how market control spread, and the damage done as educational reform for financial gain corrodes healthy relationships in learning and inequality increases. Young people are too often excluded from the politics of neoliberal schooling, because behavior and discipline policies focus on instruction, control, and compliance. In contemporary times, schools are forced to compete in global markets that measure performance in everything, including how the young conduct themselves in the classroom, in the playground, in the canteen, and on the sports oval.

This is both dangerous and damaging, as the erosion of the democratic purposes of education, and further demoralization, lead to further alienation, oppression, deficit ideologies, intolerance of difference, and exclusion from school. If the education policy process is to be properly informed and sustainable then it needs to access the perspectives of those most directly affected by schooling (Smyth, 2006, p. 33) and seek to collaborate with the school community, "enlist[ing] all players" (Slee, 1992, p. 195), rather than follow the incentives of the market.

The next chapter of this book will focus on tracing the historical, evolving, and revolving patterns and cycles of school behavior and discipline policies and practices from 16th-century Europe through to 21st-century Australia using a genealogical approach. This process unfolds reoccurring tectonic shifts and patterns across time, exposing approaches, assumptions, and belief systems that linger and return.

References

Apple, M. W. (1999). Freire, neo-liberalism and education. *Discourse: Studies in the Cultural Politics of Education, 20*(1), 5–20.

Apple, M. W. (2015). Reframing the question of whether education can change society. *Educational Theory, 65*(3), 299–315.

Aronowitz, S., & Giroux, H. (1993). *Education still under siege*. Bergin & Garvey.

Australian Law Reform Commission (ALRC). (1997). Seen and heard: Priority for children in the legal process (ALRC Report 84). https://www.alrc.gov.au/publication/seen-and-heard-priority-for-children-in-the-legal-process-alrc-report-84

Ayers, W., Ayers, R., & Dohrn, B. (2001). Introduction: Resisting zero tolerance. In W. Ayers, B. Dohn, & R. Ayers (Eds.), *Zero tolerance: Resisting the drive for punishment in our schools: A handbook for parents, students, educators, and citizens* (pp. xi–xvi). New York Press.

Ball, S. J. (2006). *Education policy and social class: The selected works of Stephen J. Ball*. Routledge.

Burawoy, M. (2009). *The extended case method: Four countries, four decades, four great transformations, and one theoretical tradition*. University of California Press.

Clarke, M., Lyon, C., Walker, E., Waltz, L., Collet-Sabé, J., & Pritchard, K. (2021). The banality of education policy: Discipline as extensive evil in the neoliberal era. *Power and Education, 13*(3), 187–204.

Connell, R. (2013). The neoliberal cascade and education: An essay on the market agenda and its consequences. *Critical Studies in Education, 54*(2), 99–112.

Connell, R., & Dados, N. (2014). Where in the world does neoliberalism come from? The market agenda in southern perspective. *Theory & Society, 43*(2), 117–138. http://doi.org/10.1007/s11186-014-9212-9

Down, B. (2016). Rethinking mis/behaviour in schools: From "youth as a problem" to the "relational school." In A. M. Sullivan, B. Johnson, & B. Lucas (Eds.), *Challenging dominant views on student behaviour at school: Answering back* (pp. 77–95). Springer.

Down, B., & Choules, K. (2017). Towards a pedagogy of personalisation: What can we learn from students? *Curriculum Perspectives, 37*, 135–145.

Fielding, M., & Moss, P. (2011). *Radical education and the common school: A democratic alternative*. Routledge.

Fine, M., & Smith, K. (2001). Zero tolerance: Reflections on a policy that won't die. In W. Ayers, B. Dohen, & R. Ayers (Eds.), *Zero tolerance: Resisting the drive for punishment: A handbook for parents, students, educators, and citizens* (pp. 256–263). New York Press.

Foucault, M. (1979). *Discipline and punish: The birth of the prison* (A. Sheridan, Trans.). Peregrine. (Original work published 1975).

Freire, P. (2004). *Pedagogy of indignation*. Paradigm.

Freire, P. (2005). *Pedagogy of the oppressed* (M. B. Ramos, Trans.). Continuum. (Original work published 1970).

Fromm, E. (1956). *The art of loving*. Open Road Integrated Media.

Gillies, V. (2011). Social and emotional pedagogies: Critiquing the new orthodoxy of emotion in classroom behaviour management. *British Journal of Sociology of Education, 32*(2), 185–202. https://doi.org/10.1080/01425692.2011.547305.

Gillies, V. (2016). *Pushed to the edge: Inclusion and behaviour support in schools*. Policy Press.

Giroux, H. (2018). When schools become dead zones of the imagination: A critical pedagogy manifesto. In K. J. Saltman & A. J. Means (Eds.), *The Wiley handbook of global educational reform* (pp. 503–515). John Wiley & Sons.

Giroux, H. (2019). Toward a pedagogy of educated hope under casino capitalism. *Pedagogía y Saberes, 50*, 147–151.

Giroux, H., & Paul, W. (2022, October 16). Educators and critical pedagogy: An antidote to authoritarianism. Canadian Dimension. https://canadiandimension.com/articles/view/educators-and-critical-pedagogy-an-antidote-to-authoritarianism

Gorski, P. (2014). Poverty, economic inequality, and the impossible promise of school reform. In P. Gorski & K. Zenkov (Eds.), *The big lies of school reform: Finding better solutions for the future of public education* (pp. 129–140). Routledge.

Hancock, K., Cave., L., Christensen D., Mitrou, F., & Zubrick, S. R. (2021). Associations between developmental risk profiles, mental disorders, and student absences among primary and secondary students in Australia. *School Mental Health*, 13, 756–771. https://doi.org/10.1007/s12310-021-09443-9

Harwood, V. (2006). *Diagnosing "disorderly" children: A critique of behaviour disorder discourses*. Routledge.

Johnson, B., & Sullivan, A. (2016). Understanding and challenging dominant discourses about student behaviour at school. In A. M. Sullivan, B. Johnson & B. Lucas (Eds.), *Challenging dominant views on student behaviour at school: Answering back* (pp. 27–43). Springer.

Kincheloe, J. L. (2007). Critical pedagogy in the twenty-first century: Evolution for survival. In P. McLaren & J. L. Kincheloe (Eds.), *Critical pedagogy: Where are we now?* (pp. 9–42). Peter Lang.

Knight, T. (1991). Democratic schooling: Basic for a school code of behaviour. In M. N. Lovegrove & R. Lewis (Eds.), *Classroom discipline* (pp. 117–144). Longman Cheshire.

Knight, T. (1997). Schools, delinquency and youth culture. In A. Borowski & I. O. Connor (Eds.), *Juvenile crime, justice and corrections* (pp. 79–97). Longman.

Kress, T. M. (2011). Inside the "thick wrapper" of critical pedagogy and research. *International Journal of Qualitative Studies in Education*, 24(3), 261–266.

Ladson-Billings, G. (2014). The pedagogy of poverty: The big lies about poor children. In P. Gorski & K. Zenkov (Eds.), *The big lies of school reform: Finding better solutions for the future of public education* (pp. 7–16). Routledge.

Lawrence, D., Dawson, V., Houghton, S., Goodsell, B., & Sawyer, M. G. (2019). Impact of mental disorders on attendance at school. *Australian Journal of Education*, 63(1), 5–21.

Lawrence, D., Hafekost, J., Johnson, S. E., Saw, S., Buckingham, W. J., Sawyer, M. G., . . . Zubrick, S. R. (2016). Key findings from the second Australian Child and Adolescent Survey of Mental Health and Wellbeing. *Australian and New Zealand Journal of Psychiatry*, 50, 876–886.

Leistyna, P. (2007). Neoliberal no-sense. In P. McLaren & J. L. Kincheloe (Eds.), *Critical pedagogy: Where are we now?* (pp. 97–123). Peter Lang.

Lingard, B., Knight, J., & Porter, P. (1995). Restructuring Australian schooling: Changing conceptions of top-down and bottom-up reforms. In B. Limerick & H. Nielsen (Eds.), *School and community relations: Participation, policy and practices* (pp. 81–99). Harcourt Brace.

McDonald, K., Keddie, A., Blackmore, J., Mahoney, C., Wilkinson, J. Gobby, B., Niesche, R., & Eacott, S. (2023). School autonomy reform and social justice: A policy overview of Australian public education (1970s to present). *Australian Educational Researcher*, 50, 307–327.

Mills, C. W. (1971). *The sociological imagination*. Penguin Books. (Original work published 1959).

Mills, M., & Pini, B. (2015). Punishing kids: The rise of the "boot camp." *International Journal of Inclusive Education*, 19(3), 270–284.

Nikolakaki, M. (2012). Critical pedagogy in the new dark ages: Challenges and possibilities: An introduction. In M. Nikolakaki (Ed.), *Critical pedagogy in the new dark ages: Challenges and possibilities* (pp. 3–31). Peter Lang.

OECD. (2023). *Education policy outlook in Australia* (OECD Education Policy Perspectives, No. 67). OECD Publishing. https://doi.org/10.1787/ce7a0965-en

Reay, D. (2017). *Miseducation: Inequality, education and the working classes*. Policy Press.

Reay, D. (2022). Lessons from abroad: How can we achieve a socially just educational system? *Irish Educational Studies, 41*(3), 425–440. https://doi.org/10.1080/03323315.2022.2085766

Rizvi, F., & Lingard, B. (2006). Globalization and the changing nature of the OECD's educational work. In H. Lauder, P. Brown, J. A. Dillabough, & A. H. Halsey (Eds.), *Education, globalization and social change* (pp. 247–260). Oxford University Press.

Rizvi, F., Lingard, B., & Rinne, R. (2022). Reimagining globalization and education: An introduction. In F. Rizvi, B. Lingard, & R. Rinne (Eds.), *Reimagining globalization and education* (pp. 1–10). Routledge. https://doi.org/10.4324/9781003207528-1

Sahlberg, P. (2021). *Finnish lessons: What can the world learn from educational change in Finland* (3rd ed.). Teachers College Press.

Senate, Education and Employment References Committee. (2023). *The issue of increasing disruption in Australian school classrooms: Interim report*. Commonwealth of Australia.

Senate, Education and Employment References Committee. (2024). *The issue of increasing disruption in Australian school classrooms: Final report*. Commonwealth of Australia.

Slee, R. (1992). Reforms and ravines: Diminishing risk in schools through systematic change. In R. Slee (Ed.), *Discipline in Australian public education: Changing policy and practice* (pp. 177–198). Australian Council for Educational Research.

Slee, R. (2011). *The irregular school: Exclusion, schooling, and inclusive education*. Routledge.

Smyth, J. (2006). Researching teachers working with young adolescents: Implications for ethnographic research. *Ethnography and Education, 1*(1), 31–51.

Smyth, J. (2011). *Critical pedagogy for social justice*. Continuum International Publishing Group.

Smyth, J. (2019a). Revisiting critical reflective practice in neoliberal times. In S. Chitin & J. P. Portelli (Eds.), *Confronting education policy in neoliberal times: International perspectives* (pp. 25–39). Routledge.

Smyth, J. (2019b). The socially just school: Transforming young lives. In K. J. Saltman & A. J. Means (Eds.), *The Wiley handbook of global educational reform* (pp. 467–487). John Wiley & Sons.

Smyth, J. (2020). A critical pedagogy of working-class schooling. In S. Steinberg & B. Down (Eds.), *The Sage handbook of critical pedagogies* (pp. 681–693). Sage.

Smyth, J., Down, B., McInerney, P., & Hattam, R. (2014). *Doing critical educational research: A conversation with the research of John Smyth*. Peter Lang.

Smyth, J., & McInerney, P. (2007). *Teachers in the middle: Reclaiming the wasteland of the adolescent years of schooling*. Peter Lang.

Smyth, J., & Wrigley, T. (2013). *Living on the edge: Rethinking poverty, class and schooling*. Peter Lang.

Welch, A. (2007). Making education policy. In R. Connell (Ed.), *Education, change and society* (pp. 1–33). Oxford University Press.

World Economic Forum. (2020). *Schools of the future: Defining new models of education for the Fourth Industrial Revolution*.

Zhang, M. (2022). Neoliberalism, critical literacy, and the everyday: A post-qual informed multi-genre inquiry. *Journal of Language & Literacy Education, 18*(2), 1–24.

· 3 ·

THE TROUBLING AND CYCLIC HISTORICAL CONTEXT

Introduction

This chapter focuses on the historical and cultural origins, bonds, and conditions shaping society to investigate "the breaks, discontinuities, and tensions" (Giroux, 1983, p. 36) of discipline policies in schools. As "history is always there, troubling and cyclical" (Saul, 2006, p. 27) the purpose of this chapter is to trace historical contexts and evolutions of contemporary discipline policies. To do this work, I lean on a genealogical approach, based on the work of Tamboukou (1999, 2016) and identify and expose major shifts, moves, and agendas in the ongoing policy-making process (Ball, 2021, p. 12). By tracking the recursive nature of these policy shifts and their implementation, it is possible to question why they happened the way that they did, socially, politically, and culturally, at different historical moments (Tamboukou, 1999, p. 204). This process exposes patterns and discourses that return, persist, and continue to linger during neoliberal times in education.

Genealogical Unfolding of the Shifting Sands of Time

> Time has ceased to be linear, with life events and memories in a chronological row, like beads on a string. You will understand it later, perhaps, this warping or folding of time. (Atwood, 2023, p. 213)

In his section, I want to say something about the methods chosen to trace the historical and genealogical evolution of discipline policy. As the ebbs and flows of these policies are not linear nor chronological, I have avoided date lines to "uncover" the political and cultural shifts and patterns, and instead use the image of the unfolding of time found in the conversations of Serres and Latour (1995). As Meredyth and Tyler (1993) explain, a genealogical approach is interested in making the "present landscape strange" and less familiar, breaking away from the usual objective rationale scientific search for "origins and foundations" (p. 4). This is not a neutral choice, but rather an activist one, as I search and "recognize what has been unlearned and what has been purposely forgotten or rewritten" (Giroux, 2023). Thinking through the past and "examining the sedimented histories" (Giroux, 1983, p. xiv) or pleats folded upon themselves and sometimes pressed into place in need of un-pleating (Serres & Latour, 1995 p. 65), time does not flow but "percolates," and some events and aspects "pass through" the weave or sieve, whilst others do not (p. 58).

An example of the unfolding of time and genealogical exposure of events described above can be found in Groundwater-Smith et al.'s (2003) brief history of secondary schooling in Australia. These authors highlight various developmental theories applied to young people that are founded on "scientific" ideas that emerged from the United States, especially the work of pioneering psychologist Granville Stanley Hall in 1916. Having borrowed from the genetically determined discourse of German writers Goethe and Schiller, G. Stanley Hall continued to emphasize "storm and stress." This explanation of student behavior has emerged again in Australia, for example, in the work of Biddulph (1984, 1997) and Lillico (2000, 2001), whose writing and consultancy work have focused on the physical changes that accompanied puberty to exaggerate the hormonal influence on "the emotional and behavioural" (Groundwater-Smith et al., 2003, p. 57).

In returning to the "folded handkerchief" image of Serres and Latour (1995), where some aspects of the past are folded into the present, and others of the past are farther away, those events and circumstances in the history of discipline policies are not only unraveled, but also interpreted as "polychromic, multitemporal, and reveal a time that is gathered together, with multiple pleats" (Serres & Latour, 1995, p. 60).

Another of these "pleats" can be found in the research of Luke (1989), as she traces pedagogy, printing, and Protestantism in 16th-century Europe. She explains that not only did book learning become part of daily life during this time but also accompanied with "state legislated school ordinances, prescribed curricula and instructional methods for schoolmasters" (p. 138). This disciplinary discourse appears again in contemporary times with an educational culture of standardized curricula, testing, school rules, consequences, teacher advisory manuals, and surveillance, all of which "eliminate diversity and promote uniformity of teaching and learning" (Luke, 1989, p. 138).

Weaver and Morris (2022), in describing Michel Serres' pedagogical life's work, conclude that his main philosophical message was to "invent new ways of seeing and being" as patterns emerged and developed again over time (p. 351). Using the combination of a genealogical approach and invoking Michel Serres' ways of "seeing and being," this chapter will now focus on these major shifts (named "tectonic" shifts), to trace and identify the history of discipline policies, politically, culturally, and socially. These shifts are reinforced by a discussion about the discourses that have returned and those that never really went away. These are discourses that linger and persist, even if disguised as "vocabulary shifts" (Bessant et al., 2017, p. 1).

Evolving Historical Tectonic Shifts

> Rather than approach the task with a microscope, we need magnification with wide-angle lenses to increase our peripheral or lateral vision to engage with the "messy realities" of history and policy. (Slee, 1995, p. 10)

In concentrating on the past and revealing the driving forces into the consciousness of the present (Foley, 2002, p. 482), those patterns and events that have influenced discipline policies become apparent, exposing the recursive nature of discourses at different historical moments, redirecting attention to local contexts and specific actions. They are complex and messy sites, these historical movements or shifts in discourse that collide (Slee, 2016, p. 73). I label these shifts "tectonic" (using "wide-angle lenses") (T1–T7), beginning from 16th-century Europe and tracing, in a genealogical and unfolding manner, through to school systems in contemporary Australia. These discursive shifts have not operated in isolation, nor have they been enacted independent of global political and systemic systems through time, because they often overlap and intertwine. The first discursive shift goes as far back as I can find on the topic of discipline policy in relation to contemporary times and comes from an essay from La Boétie (1975).

T1 Obedient Servitude to Religious Pastoral

In the 1550 essay, *The discourse of voluntary servitude*, La Boétie (1975) acknowledges the foundations of tyranny and the politics of obedience. La Boétie questions servitude to tyrants and suggests it is fostered when people are raised in subjection and trained to adore rulers. Nevertheless, he explains, "while freedom is forgotten by many, there are always some who will never submit" (p. 55). There will always be a struggle for freedom. Almost two centuries after La Boétie, I have discovered instructions extracted from a 1748 German child-rearing manual (Sulzer, as cited in Miller, 1990) that point to the accepted version of "obedience" and compliance at this time: "Persons of high estate who are destined to rule whole nations must learn the art of governance by way of first learning obedience" (Sulzer, as cited in Miller, 1990, p. 12).

Puritan values of obedience were readily adopted during the 16th-century Reformation (Olssen, 1999, p. 162) and, being Calvinist in character, were based on "ideal capitalist, quasi-militaristic, patriarchal social relations and industrial order" (Preston & Symes, 1992, p. 40). The word "discipline" derives from Medieval Latin and is connected to the word "disciple" (Moore, 2004, p. 396). The Protestant religion "gave rise to a new spirit of individualism, in which, each individual could communicate directly with God and was solely responsible for his or her salvation" (Olssen, 1999, p. 162).

As school systems expanded throughout Europe during this time, churches became the "instruments for the intensification and dissemination of Christian spiritual discipline and pastoral guidance," which reached its apex under 18th-century "pietism" (Olssen, 1999, p. 168). These modes of operation continued infiltrating into daily life and the school, "through its architecture, pedagogy, and administration" (Olssen, 1999, p. 169).

T2 Pastoral and the Individual

The expansion of the European empire and the Enlightenment belief in progress and theories of natural law (Rose, 1990, p. 217) encouraged the idea that "the individual was master of their fate" (Olssen, 1999, p. 162). The rise of individualism, linked to Protestantism, Romanticism, and the growth of the bureaucratic idea of governmentalization (Rose, 1990; Preston & Symes, 1992) culminated in the simultaneous emergence of both supervision and administration. Christian pastoral pedagogy (Hunter, 1994, p. 65) also meant that those pupils who did not conform were considered "maladjusted" and were therefore punished as "a technique for the coercion of individuals" (Foucault, 1979, p. 131).

The "power to punish" (Foucault, 1979, p. 82) was thereafter exercised more deeply into the social body "in the form of habits in behaviour" (p. 131) as the disciplinary society gradually extended the mechanisms of discipline, making it easier to forge a controlled, docile working student (Foucault, 1979, p. 209). Throughout England, as Smith (1991) explains, "mass schooling came into being at least partly as a response to the problem of how to regulate large numbers of children appearing in cities as a product of industrialisation" (p. 40). Consequently, there was even greater surveillance (Harber, 2004, p. 71; Tait, 2013, p. 271), and thereafter, a preparation for subordinate roles in the workplace within wider society to control the poor and disadvantaged (Connell et al., 1982, p. 60).

As European colonialism was transported around the globe, so too were world views, systems and logics of education more widely disseminated, especially from Great Britain, Spain, and the Netherlands. As explained in the previous section, these structures were based on disciplinary connotations associated with dealing with refractory conduct (Preston & Symes, 1992, p. 33). Australia, as a colonial nation, embraced pastoral pedagogy "as its population was regarded, with its convict origins, as recalcitrant" (Preston & Symes, 1992, p. 41) and therefore in need of Christian moral guidance.

T3 Mass Schooling in Australia

> The phenomenon of mass, compulsory elementary schooling documented one encounter between the Australian family and the State, leaving a unique record for historians. (Theobald, 1990, p. viv)

It is no surprise that Australia, as a British colony (Tait, 2013, p. 273), inherited many truths and beliefs concerning discipline in schools described in the sections above. Throughout the 19th century, much of Australia's schooling "just happened, rather than being planned" (Lovat, 2004, p. 108). The domination of Australian society "by those of Anglo Celtic descent from the 1850's to the 1950s, allowed the role of schools in equipping young people for citizenship to be constructed in narrowly, and British, patriotic terms" (Vick, 2004, p. 75). Schools in Australia also popped up in all sorts of buildings—"churches, houses, shops, barns, sheds, huts"—containing "blackboards, standardised desks, globes, wall charts, maps and illustrations, sand trays" (p. 58). As described earlier, the responses to refractory conduct combined with compulsory school attendance became cemented with "economic and political purposes" (p. 58).

During these times of mass compulsory education, there was a melding together of "middle-class judgements about working-class families" (Vick, 2004, p. 68), resulting in certain groups of young people being either excluded or considered to have "failed" schooling and having therefore "to find work on the farm, in the factory, on the shopfloor, or in domestic labour" (Slee, 2018, p. 6). By the late 20th century, many organizations took a vested interest in education including "employers, parents, Catholic education systems, independent private schools, and teachers" (Vick, 2004, p. 73).

T4 School Tone and Good Example

> Discipline policies in Australian public education tend to be behaviourist in conception and practice. (Slee, 1995, p. 3)

Between the 1920s and 1930s, the interwar years in Australia, a strong education guidance movement was adopted from the United States with an emphasis on psychology to intervene and remediate maladjusted problem children and correct their deficiencies (Wright, 2010). Thus, by the 1950s in Western Australian schools, pastoral care, and to some degree the Protestant church philosophy, underpinned by notions of responsibility and personal development, was in large part a response to the concern about corporal punishment being abolished by law elsewhere at the time, such as throughout Western Europe.

This shift from external control and punishment to a greater emphasis on the individual and self-esteem became apparent in 1959, when the Western Australian Education Department issued a 10-page statement, "Discipline in the secondary school and classroom." This was a supplement to the *Education Circular* (Figure 3.1), in which the term "discipline" was used to "signify the degree of order or organization within a group which works, or is required to work, for a particular purpose" (WAED, 1959, p. 20). The influence and co-operation of all staff members was accentuated in this document as one of the most important factors in determining "school tone" (p. 23). The intent was to eliminate disciplinary problems: "a cardinal principle in the development of good tone and discipline is that positive attitudes are developed through

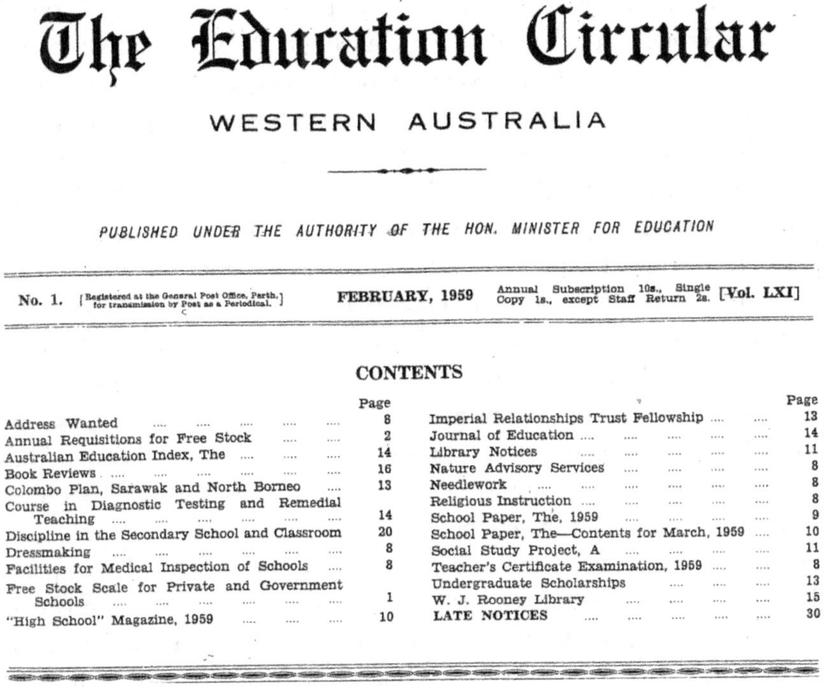

THE TROUBLING AND CYCLIC HISTORICAL CONTEXT

Figure 3.1: *The Education Circular*, February 1959

experiences that are meaningful and satisfying" (p. 21). Good tone, in turn, became defined as deriving from good example: "from the absorption of the energies of pupils in constructive learning activities which hold their interests, and from the development of self-discipline through progressively increasing responsibility" (p. 29). From this time onwards corporal punishment was discouraged and it was eventually abolished in public schools in 1987.

T5 Pastoral Care, Whole of School Approach, and Suspension

Historically, Western Australian high schools have evolved from a system where order was secured by coercion. Discipline was maintained almost exclusively by rules and regulations enforced by penalties. While many of these penalties—corporal punishment, detention and the like—are still employed in schools, their automatic implementation for breaches of school rules ought to be relatively rare occurrences thanks to a *better understanding of the needs and developmental phases of the child.* (WAED, 1972, p. 134, emphasis added)

In 1967, the Western Australian Education Department established a committee under the chairmanship of the Director-General, H. W. Dettman, to investigate and report on the future organization of secondary education. It was the first time that the aims and the role of schools were to be explicitly detailed (Hyde, 1992, p. 63). This represented the most extensive government enquiry into student discipline in Australia (Slee, 1995, p. 123) and all secondary schools in Western Australia (approximately 60) were surveyed regarding their rates of suspension and their efficacy and discipline. This investigation, of which an excerpt is shared above, culminated in the Dettman Report, *Discipline in secondary schools in Western Australia* (WAED, 1972), totaling 376 pages with 43 recommendations.

Contained within the Dettman Report were 78 case studies of "deviant behavior" from 28 schools. Five of the recommendations related to punishment, significantly the phasing out of corporal punishment (WAED, 1972, p. 3). In its place, specific reference was made to fostering pastoral care and moral education because "detachment in school may be a symptom of the larger picture of psychological discontent rather than a specific malfunction of school operation" (p. 110). To assist the "alienated adolescent, engulfed with feelings of mistrust and misfortune," it recommended "small group instruction or individual counselling" (p. 111). Other reforms recommended included curriculum changes to focus on "human relations lessons, more guidance officers and support staff for counselling, and sub school structures for larger secondary schools" (Hyde, 1992, p. 63).

In 1980, at the Western Australian secondary school principals conference, great concern was expressed regarding disruptive behaviors of students. Practical resolutions were sought and "a proposal was made to the Education Department for a systemwide series of in-service courses for teachers on behaviour management" (Hyde, 1992, p. 70). As a result, a "whole-of-school approach" was adopted throughout many government schools in Western Australia.

By 1984, the Committee of Inquiry into Education in Western Australia (from here on known as the Beazley Inquiry), recommended that government schools appoint chaplains for pastoral care and counseling (Rec. 77) and by 1985 the "Chaplaincy in Schools" program was established. The Beazley Report also recognized the significance of "care and self-esteem for all who work in schools, and in particular, for students" (Committee of Inquiry into Education in WA, p. 149). The committee used a discussion paper titled *The provision of caring environments in secondary school* (WAED) & Caring School Environment Committee, 1982) to develop seven of its own recommendations (pp. 70–77) based on the need for "caring environments" in secondary schools.

Following the Beazley Report, a report on disruptive behavior in schools in Western Australia was commissioned by the Ministry of Education (from here on known as the Louden Report (WAED, 1985). The Louden Report also encouraged schools to adopt more caring environments, with Recommendation 18 requesting that "resources be made available for the development of a school-wide caring environment" (p. 33).

Guidelines for School Discipline 1988

Ironically, the Western Australian *Education* Amendment Act 1982 empowered the Minister of Education to suspend or exclude disruptive students, where "the conduct and behaviour of a child" was "not conducive to the good order and proper management of the Government school" (Bain & Macpherson, 1990, p. 110). During this same period, as Hyde (1992, pp. 71–72) explains, the taskforce charged "with the responsibility for examining pastoral care in terms of concept, definition and practice" was "disbanded" as the newly elected state government established the Beazley Inquiry (Hyde, 1992, p. 71). The Beazley committee had been made aware that disruptive behavior was still a significant problem for many schools and "the use of formalized within-school suspensions and suspensions from school were proposed" (Hyde, 1992, p. 72). The committee required "schools [to] develop and make public their policy on care and discipline," and also recommended "the establishment of off-site withdrawal centres for severely disruptive students" (Rec. 271) (as cited in Hyde, 1992, p. 72). The Louden Report also recommended that schools establish in-school suspension for disruptive students and the use of "time out" rooms as a sanction (WAED, 1985), consistent with Glasser's (1969, 1975) therapy model.

In mid-1987, corporal punishment was formally abolished in Western Australian state schools, and the newly restructured Ministry of Education released *Guidelines for student exclusion panels* in 1987 and *Guidelines for school discipline* in 1988. Under the new *School Education Act 1999*, the function of teachers was "to supervise students and to maintain proper order and discipline on their part" (section 64(1)(e), principals were responsible for the safety and welfare of students and the Director General was responsible for determining, implementing, and monitoring the standard of education and care provided to students (Murphy, 2014, p. 15).

Devolution and the Management of "At Risk" Students

The devolution of responsibility, set in motion earlier with the Beazley Report, was reinforced by the Western Australian Education Department's 1996–1998

Strategic Plan (WAED, 1995), which advised each school to develop and implement a School Development Plan to have "more scope for decision making at a school level" (Objective 3). The Strategic Plan for Government Schools Education, 1998–2000 (WAED, 1997) that followed, listed specific targets as indicators of progress for Objective 3. This included the target that "by January 1999, *all schools* will be implementing procedures for effectively resolving conflict at the school level" (p. 14, emphasis added).

One of the five major strategies linked to Objective 3 through operational and school planning was "Students at Educational Risk." This strategy was named *Making the Difference* and was to be the first official "Behaviour Management in Schools Policy" (WAED, 1998a, 1998b). This strategy listed responsibilities of principals, classroom teachers, and district directors, and included "guidelines for the isolation of students with disruptive behaviour' (Sec 2). In addition, "support materials" for attention deficit/hyperactivity disorder and violence, bullying, and harassment prevention (Sec. 4) were provided, plus sample "Behaviour Management Plans" and "Codes of Behaviour" (Sec. 6), including the example: "obey directions from staff at all times" (WAED, 1998b, p. 7).

An updated Behavior Management Policy was introduced into Western Australian secondary schools at the beginning of 2001, accompanied by the new *School Education Act 1999*. Section 4.2 of the 2001 Behaviour Management Policy (WADET, 2001) provides explicit details and procedures to be followed, including "detaining students after school," "withdrawal of students from school activities," "suspension of a student from school," "exclusion orders," and "physical restraint of students" (p. 20). Over half of the policy content (Sec 8, Appendices, pp. 22–39), related to suspensions and exclusions of students. This policy was mandated in all government schools by 2002 and at the base of each of the first 20 pages was the footnote:

> All policy and procedural statements contained within this document are lawful orders for the purpose of section 80 (a) of the Public Sector Management Act 1994 (W.A.) and therefore to be observed by all Department of Education and Training employees.

T6 Recording, Monitoring and Reporting Student Behavior

The 1998 Behavior Management in Schools Policy (WAED, 1998b) listed additional requirements for record keeping, including records of the use of isolation rooms as a strategy (Sec. 2, p. 1), in which "the name of student, analysis of their disruptive behavior, log of times, names of supervisors, detail of student whilst in isolation and the overall effect of isolation as a modifier of the students' behaviour" (p. 1) all had to be recorded. These requirements were followed by an updated policy (WADET, 2001) which announced that "teaching staff must keep records of student behaviour," also including the name of the student, dates, and times; and in addition, a "description of the behaviour, reasons for selecting management strategies and detail of the use of management strategies" (p. 5). In addition, individual Behavior Management Plans had to "be documented to make clear the behavioural issues being addressed, desired outcomes, strategies to be used and the effectiveness of the strategies" (p. 5). Other record keeping included listing any students who were "detained after school" or "withdrawn from school activities" (pp. 6–7).

It is no surprise, therefore, that the Western Australian Education Department contracted RM Asia-Pacific Pty Ltd in the year 2000 to develop a web-based Student Information System (SIS) as a mechanism for recording, monitoring, and reporting on student behavior and attendance in all government schools. The updated behavior policy (WADET, 2008a) continued to insist that *all* school staff were required to "demonstrate accountability for evidence-based decision making, reporting and referral to appropriate support, and record keeping" (p. 4), ensuring that schools swiftly sought out and embraced the use of SIS as a data system, preferred, financed, and endorsed by the Western Australian Education Department.

The Auditor General's report on behavior management policy throughout Western Australian schools (Murphy, 2014) noted that, "whilst SIS can be used to record positive and negative behaviour data for analysis, the Department of Education only requires schools to record negative behaviour in relation to suspending or excluding students" (p. 18). The suspension data from Western Australian government schools during the time from the first official behavior management policy through to 2009 shows that students were removed from schools in alarming numbers. For example, in 1994 there were 1630 student suspensions in Western Australian government schools (House of Representatives, Standing Committee on Employment, Education and Training, 1996, p. 12) and yet only three years later, in 1997, as monitoring systems and behavior management strategies became more prevalent, more than 12,000 students were suspended (Carpenter, 2003). By 2006, 10,000 out of a total of 250,000 students were suspended and yet the Western Australian Education Department continued to claim that the additional funding was helping to improve student behavior and that the increase in suspensions was "due to more accurate reporting of incidents" (WADET, 2007). By 2007, 10,536 students were suspended from a total of 252,000 students (WADET 2008c) and the Minister of Education stated that this increase was because "considerable toughening-up has already occurred" and that suspensions had been "streamlined" so that they could be sped up (p. 1).

The SIS system assisted in the streamlining of student suspensions, as confirmed in 2008 when 11,417 students were suspended (Hiatt, 2009). In 2009, suspensions continued to increase (12,529). The Director General, however, continued to argue that this was due to a "tougher stance taken on disruptive behaviour" and "because more than half (57.2%) of those students had only been suspended once, that they had learned their lesson" (WADET, 2010).

T7 Diagnosis, Behavior Modification, and Private Enterprise

Research from de Jong (2005) outlined "A framework of principles and best practice for managing student behaviour in the Australian education context" and reported that a lack of discipline had been a major concern throughout Australian schools for the 30 years prior (p. 353). From 2003 to 2004, de Jong undertook the role of principal researcher for the "Student Behaviour Management Project," a taskforce that was formed to provide Australian education ministers "with advice on programs that exhibit best practice" (p. 354). What is prominent in this report are the individual "diagnostic assessments" based on promoting a "psychological health culture" and Individual Education Programs (p. 363). The five models of student behavior management that de Jong (2005) stated "allied to good practice in Australia" (p. 365) were William Glasser's "Choice Theory," Edward Carr et al.'s "Positive Behaviour Support," Ed Ford's "Responsible Thinking Process," restorative justice, Rudolf Dreikurs's "Democratic Discipline Model," and Lee and Marlene Canter's "Assertive Discipline Model" (pp. 365–366).

Angus et al.'s (2010) Pipeline Project reported that "regular classrooms now contain increased numbers of children who are difficult to teach, while at the same time schools are expected to achieve higher educational standards" (p. 2). An emphasis on measuring standards both nationally (NAPLAN) and internationally (OECD's PISA) meant that the student not performing well in high-stakes tests are perceived to be a problem and "substantial numbers of children attending school are thought to have disorders" (Angus et al., 2010, p. 3). Managing disruptive students, Angus et al. (2010) argue, is the "core business for teachers" (p. 11).

Private Enterprise and Behavior Management

An example of the impact of private enterprise infiltrating schools was an emphasis on Classroom Management Skills (CMS) distributed into all Western Australian government schools as part of the $AUS 17 million Behavior Management and Discipline Strategy 2001–2007. This trend continued as part of the Enterprise Bargaining Agreements (in 2006, 2008, 2011, 2021) with the State School Teachers' Union of WA, and was consolidated when universities incorporated CMS into teacher training courses. CMS professional development was distributed throughout the state to "ensure[s] that education administrators and teachers:

- develop excellent, practical strategies for handling behavioral issues
- understand their rights and duties in relation to behavior management
- are aware of the procedures in place to call on the police as necessary
- are provided with advice about what to do (i.e., move-on notices, violence restraining orders, pressing charges, etc.)" (Education Workforce Initiatives Ministerial Taskforce, 2007, p. 56).

CMS training was based on Michael Fullan's (1983) *The meaning of educational change*, modeled on Hunter and Russell's (1990) *Mastering coaching and supervision*, implemented by Bennett and Smilanich's (1994) *Classroom management*, and followed by McDonald's (2010) *Classroom management*. The privatization of systemic educational reform provided markets for these authors and consultants to continue publishing manuals, tools, and techniques in schools and universities throughout Western Australia. McDonald's (2010) *Classroom management*, for example, is now in its third edition (McDonald, 2019) and links with the seven Australian Institute of Teaching and School Leadership standards. It has new content on neuroscience and includes the Positive Learning Framework model. McDonald's national success in marketing *Classroom management* has also resulted in his appointment as a "subject matter expert," "guiding teachers to deliver routines, strategies and approaches" in an Australian government $3.5 million "Engaged Classrooms" project. The launch of this project coincided with the OECD's (2023) report on school improvement, which stated that "the disciplinary climate in schools in Australia was among the least favorable in the OECD" and "a smaller share of Australian teachers than their peers across the OECD reported feeling prepared for, or capable of, managing disruptive classroom behaviour" (p. 23). To address high teacher turnover, the OECD report recommended that "teacher development in classroom management and student behaviour management" should "drive improvement in school disciplinary climate" (p. 24).

Ecclestone (2017) argues that, when educational entrepreneurs' behavior and discipline reform agendas align with "a favoured approach for government-funded profit," they also have a "wider influence in government policy and public thinking" (p. 54). Tom Bennett, another successful entrepreneur in behavior reform in Australia, was behavior advisor for the United Kingdom's government from 2015. Bennett's (2017) report on behavior reveals some of his charismatic, moral, and evangelical leanings:

> Behavior flows from character, intentions, and circumstances. School leaders should rightly aim to influence student character and attitudes. [. . .]
>
> It is the duty of every adult to help create in students the habit of self-restraint or self-regulation. This must be mastered before students can consider themselves to be truly free. [. . .] Compliance is only one of several rungs on a behavioural ladder we hope all our students will climb, but it is a necessary one to achieve first. Once obtained, students can then be supported into true autonomy and independence, where they reliably and consciously make wise and civil decisions without supervision or restraint. (pp. 13, 33)

Bennett's business organization "researchED" has established companies all over the world, including Australia. The keynote speakers at his launch in Australia in 2022 included school principal Katharine Birbalsingh (considered to be the strictest), and "cognitive load theorist" John Sweller. As Ecclestone (2017) explains, "contemporary evangelical practitioners use populist adaptions" of the Christian and pastoral foundations noted in earlier sections of this chapter by "combining psychological ideas and practices and interweaving them with goals to raise success, achievement, motivation and engagement" (p. 54). Connected to Bennett's organization researchEd is evidence-based "school improvement" company "EDvance," founded by the Fogarty Foundation in 2012 in Western Australia. The role of this company was to "support schools in challenging communities" and to "play an important role in an education system where schools are increasingly more autonomous" (https://fogartyedvance.au/). EDvance continues to be funded by the Western Australian Education Department and Catholic Education Western Australia and their chosen "delivery partner" for the program being the Knowledge Society (https://knowledgesociety.com.au). The Knowledge Society has central offices based in the Australian capital cities of Perth and Sydney claiming to "build intellectual capital" and assisting "school systems and governments achieve gains in student learning outcomes," with their "deep knowledge base for improvement." This, Ecclestone (2017) argues, is the emotive, soothing "charisma" that "sells interventions" (p. 54).

Behavior Centers & CARE Schools

In 2007, the Western Australian Minister of Education announced the trialing of three specialist behavior centers for "violent and disruptive high school students" (Education Workforce Initiatives Ministerial Taskforce, 2007, p. 57) and was continued as confirmed in the Department of Education's annual report (WADE, 2015a):

> The wellbeing, resilience, emotional regulation and behaviour of children and young people continue to be challenging issues [… and] changes are being made to a number of structures and services to better support and engage students, including behaviour centres. (p. 23)

In the same year, the Western Australian Department of Education (WADE, 2015b) described a culture of "high performance—high care" (p. 3), as a priority for improvement in their strategic plan (2016–2019), to "introduce alternative settings to meet the specific needs of some students" (p. 5). In 2016, the same department created a new model (WADE, 2016), in which the twelve existing behavior centers were renamed as "engagement centers," plus another two were set up in regional centers. This plan included student engagement and behavior united into one state-wide service, with an extra allocation of $20 million a year. By 2019, the behavior centers were renamed once more as "Alternative Learning Settings" to "provide alternative facilities and targeted support programs to WA school students who have been excluded or are at high risk of being excluded" (WADE, 2022, p. 30). In 2023, the Western Australian Education Department announced on their webpage, that "in addition to the existing twelve 'behaviour centres' an additional two regional ones would be established; plus, a new, small and specialised school specifically designed to meet the learning needs of severely disengaged secondary students" (WADE, 2023).

Ingram (2020) conducted an inquiry to determine the extent of financial resources available in Western Australia to address student health and wellbeing needs, and how these resources were distributed to support individual students. This report revealed that one single behavior center was allocated $18.7 million in March 2019 and that they are costly:

> The importance of engaging every student in Western Australian is paramount. However, no one formulae works in every school and the strategies for intervention

vary according to student need. With this in mind measuring the impact of funding related to the engagement of children and young people in school and learning presents some inherent difficulties and complexity. (Ingram, 2020, p. 7)

It is not surprising, therefore, that, with an escalating demand for behavior centers throughout Western Australia, they have been relabeled as "independent" schools or "academies" established under the banner of "CARE" schools (Curriculum and Re-engagement in Education) for "disengaged" youth or "young people at risk" and registered though the Western Australian Department of Education. They are sometimes affiliated with schools of religion, or youth groups, plus vocational and entrepreneurial centers. These schools are often funded via charities and large companies such as Shell Petroleum, chambers of commerce, and universities and can therefore apply for grants such as the Australian Government Capital Grants Program. They also often form partnerships with similar international schools including the United States, Asia, and Europe.

CARE schools, as an expanding privatized business, even though costly to run at around $30,000 per student (twice that for most mainstream secondary schools) (Ingram, 2020, p. 11), continue to be officially supported by state and national governments, because they are released not only from full financial burden, but also any direct responsibility for dealing with disengaged young people.

Discussion: Discipline Discourses That Linger

"Policy-as-discourse" sees policy as part of a wider system of social relations, framing what is said and thought. (Blackmore & Lauder, 2006, p. 98)

It is not possible to fit this discussion into a neat linear timeline because some practices, as revealed in the seven tectonic shifts explored in the previous section, continue spinning and repeating themselves in the historical context of behavior and discipline policies. The purpose of this section is to provide a synopsis of those policy discourses that have lingered from 16th-century Europe through to the present.

Punishment Practice 1: Compliance

Obedience, servitude, and compliance, a preoccupation from 16th-century Europe (La Boétie, 1975), returns like a whirling time warp into the present, for example, the Pipeline Project (Angus et al., 2010). This project's report declares that "teachers need to establish an *orderly* classroom environment because *disorder* leads to teacher stress" (p. 7, emphasis added). In turn, the teachers want students to:

> Start on time, prepare for the lesson, attend to what the teacher says, comply with the teacher's direction, strive to finish assigned tasks to the highest possible standard, collaborate constructively with other students when required, and work without disturbing other students when required. (Angus et al., 2010, p. 7)

Ball (1990) defines "discourse" as "what can be said and thought, but also about who can speak, when and with what authority" (p. 2). The report from Angus et al. (2010) is overt in sharing *who* and *what* can be spoken about when reporting on the trajectories of behavior, progress, and engagement with learning. That is because these pathways are measured according to "positive conduct, rule following, adhering to norms" (Frydenberg et al., 2005, p. 4). The assumption is that: "Morally driven classroom management practices are likely to produce more self-aware, morally autonomous, responsible students who conscientiously aspire to be the best that they can be at all times" (Fogelgarn & Lewis, 2015, p. 278). Fogelgarn and Lewis (2015) take the "moral high ground" a step further, when they claim, "children enter school expecting to obey authority" and, as they mature, "obedience usually morphs into compliance" (p. 289).

Punishment Practice 2: Surveillance

Harber (2004, p. 71) explains that one of the key purposes of mass systems of formal schooling in industrializing countries was control and surveillance. The idea of mass schooling was imported to Australia from Europe and the Anglo-Saxon world with a focus on "the minute subdivision of space and time, around continual surveillance, around hierarchical observation, around the examination, around the uniforms" (Tait, 2013, p. 271). This surveillance of students has returned as a disciplinary apparatus in the form of behavior management software data systems, "where a single gaze" is able to "see everything constantly" (Foucault, 1979, p. 173), for example, the Student Information System (SIS) deployed throughout Western Australian government schools. There are, however, many other software systems that continue to be vigorously and successfully marketed for student surveillance throughout the globe, even if that was not their initial function. These are powerful tools of surveillance that shape pedagogical and administrative practices (Manolev et al., 2019, p. 43).

Punishment Practice 3: Evangelism

Another astonishing pattern from the past involves the attitudes and practices of 18th-century imperialism and 19th-century evangelism returning to save the souls of "unruly" and "amoral" youth. In the February 1959 *Education Circular* to secondary schools from the Western Australian Minister for Education, a special interest was taken "in the matter of discipline and tone" and "an exceptionally good working spirit was sought" (WAED, 1959, p. 20). In more recent times, these beliefs return under the guise of protection, safety, security of "others," and the wellbeing of the "individual." For example, the Government of Western Australia's school improvement and accountability framework (WADET, 2008b) links safety and wellbeing to improving performance:

> A learning environment that is safe, caring and inclusive is also a pre-requisite for improving the standards of student achievement. It is the responsibility of schools, with system support, to establish a learning environment where students feel safe, where student behaviour is well managed, where pastoral care programs promote student wellbeing and where attendance, retention and engagement are priorities. (p. 9)

Punishment Practice 4: Isolation

Another pattern to return is the separation and isolation of students who do not perform well. In early Australian schooling, these children were "put to work" on farms and in factories (Slee, 2018. p. 6); however, in recent times they are isolated, suspended, excluded, and warehoused into institutions in a society obsessed with school improvement, measurement, outcomes, and performance. Gillies' (2016) ethnographic research demonstrates the way in which neoliberal schooling pathologizes, separates, and discriminates against disadvantaged youth via the proliferation of Behavior Support Units, pushing them to the edges and depriving them of a meaningful future in education. Five new "Secondary Behavior Centers" were introduced into Western Australian government schools as part of new exclusion procedures in the "Classroom First Strategy" (WADET, 2008a) "to manage the behaviour of the most challenging students and restore stronger discipline and standards to schools." By 2022, these centers had mushroomed across the state, outsourced to private youth or church organizations, and subsidized by government funds under the banner of Curriculum and Re-engagement in Education (CARE) centers or academies.

Punishment Practice 5: Labeling

Deficit discourses of the past, such as "deviant," were used ninety times in the Dettman Report (WAED, 1972) and have returned in the 20th century, with those young people disaffected from schooling now being labeled "at risk" or "disruptive." The first official Western Australian Government Behavior Management in Schools Policy (WAED, 1998a) provides clear guidelines for planning on the "isolation of students with disruptive behaviour" (pp. 1–2). The policy argues that isolating students is effective in managing behavior because it:

> Provide[s] students exhibiting disruptive behaviours the opportunity to cool down, and reflect on their own behaviour; ensure duty-of-care provisions for other students in the class; allow the teacher and other students in the class the opportunity to teach and learn without interference; and protect the threatened rights of class members. (p. 1)

The Western Australian *Education Amendment Act 1982* gave schools the power to suspend or exclude "disruptive students," where "the conduct and behaviour of a child" was "not conducive to the good order and proper management of the Government school" (Bain & Macpherson, 1990, p. 110). Three years later, the Louden report (WAED, 1985) on "disruptive behaviour in schools" was commissioned by the Western Australian Ministry of Education. Almost 40 years later, the Senate Education and Employment References Committee report (2024) addressed concerns about "the impact of disorderly, poorly disciplined classroom environments and school practices on students' learning, compared with their peers in more disciplined classrooms" (p. 1).

Most disruptive student behaviors in classrooms were reported as low-level in the interim version of this Senate Education and Employment References Committee report (2023) and included students "talking unnecessarily and calling out without permission; being slow to start work or follow instructions; showing a lack of respect for each other and staff; not bringing the right equipment; and using mobile devices inappropriately" (p. 3). Araujo (2005) asks if this labeling of student behavior as "disruptive" is fair because the institutionalization and organization of schools plays a "crucial role" in disaffected behavior (p. 251).

Punishment Practice 6: Pathologization

During the Enlightenment period throughout Europe a rapid dispersal of behaviorist science and cognitive psychologies "guided and counselled the way" (Usher & Edwards, 1994, p. 97), making the behavior easier to deal with than the schools' structure, pedagogy, politics, and curriculum (Slee, 1995, p. 62). This behaviorist discourse meant that "the naughty child, the fidgety child, the disengaged child" was "refashioned as the maladjusted, the troubled, the disordered and the genetically compromised" (Slee, 2011, p. 149).

Therapeutic practices have returned, with an emphasis on the cognitive and the psychological (Millei et al., 2010; Wright, 2014). For example, in the Commissioner for Children and Young People's (2019) report *Improving the odds for WA's vulnerable children and young people*, evidence garnered from experts in the field suggested that "one of the key drivers of children's development are their biology" and "children who grow up in poverty may have difficulty learning and at school: they may find it difficult to adapt, concentrate, manage their behaviour and emotions" (p. 16).

As young people's behavior is categorized under various "dis/order" labels such as attention deficit/hyperactivity disorder (ADHD) and its siblings, "conduct disorder and oppositional defiance disorder" (Slee, 2011, p. 136), plus the ever-expanding pathologies such as intermittent explosive disorder reaction, compulsive disorder, autism spectrum disorder and auditory processing disorder, then particular patterns of inclusion and exclusion are generated (Slee, 2011, p. 136). An investigative case study of diagnoses of ADHD in a secondary school in Sweden (Hjörne & Säljö, 2006), for example, confirms that "behavioural problems" were assessed as neuropsychiatric disorders and "understood in terms of brain dysfunction rather than as responses to concrete events in the school situation" (p. 614).

Conclusion

> Not everything that is faced can be changed. But nothing can be changed until it has been faced. History is not the past. It is the present. We carry our history with us. We are our history. (James Baldwin, as cited in Giroux, 2023)

In contrast to these troubling and cyclic patterns, discussed throughout this chapter, Taylor and Kearney (2018) remind us that, if our young people are to "take their place as successful twenty-first-century citizens," then "they will need an entirely new set of skills, dispositions, and understandings" (p. 100). In contrast to traditional regulated and controlling systems of conformity, obedience, and cognitive performance, students require more important skills and knowledges such as "participation, critical thinking, creativity, and innovation" (p. 100).

I have used a genealogical approach to trace the lines and folds of historical evolution of school behavior and discipline policies over time to capture and understand significant social, political, cultural, and historical patterns, interactions, and influences using seven significant discourses that I have named "tectonic shifts." The Western Australian Government's public education system's evolution of school behavior and discipline policies provided a case study of disciplinary patterns for discussion. This process has exposed a series of persistent and repetitive assumptions, beliefs, and values underpinning school discipline and behavior management discourses over time.

The purpose of this chapter has been to search for those "insights" (Taylor & Kearney, 2018, p. 88) and "fleeting possibilities" (Giroux, 1983, p. xiv) to make a difference in how we think and learn from our past, to be in the present and reshape the future. This vision requires a willingness to ask more probing kinds of questions about school discipline while struggling for a more democratic and socially just response. As Freire (2004) explains, it is important to break away and consciously engage in reflective praxis with a particular focus on historical and shifting discourses:

> Conscience of the world engenders conscience of the self, and of others in the world, and with the world. It is by acting in the world that we make ourselves. Therefore, it is by inserting ourselves into the world, not by adapting to it, that we become historical and ethical beings, capable of opting, of deciding, of breaking away. (p. 72)

In the following two chapters, I share in-depth ethnographic studies of two case study secondary schools within Western Australia to critically investigate school behavior disciplinary policies over time, past, present, and likely future. These chapters unravel common themes and frameworks collated from both case study sites that apply to not only these two particular schools, but many others worldwide.

References

Angus, M., McDonald, T., Ormand, C., Rybarcyk, R., & Taylor, A. (2010). *Pipeline project: Trajectories of classroom behaviour and academic progress: A study of student engagement with learning*. Edith Cowan University.

Araujo, M. (2005). Disruptive or disrupted? A qualitative study on the construction of indiscipline. *International Journal of Inclusive Education*, 9(3), 241–268.

Atwood, M. (2023). *Old babes in the wood*. Chatto & Windus.

Bain, A., & Macpherson, A. (1990). An examination of the system-wide use of exclusion with disruptive students. *Australia and New Zealand Journal of Developmental Disabilities*, 16(2), 109–123.

Ball, S. (1990). Introducing Monsieur Foucault. In S. J. Ball (Ed.), *Foucault and education: Disciplines and knowledge* (pp. 1–8). Routledge.

Ball, S. (2021). *The education debate* (4th ed.). Policy Press.

Bennett, B., & Smilanich, P. (1994). *Classroom management: A thinking & caring approach*. Bookation.

Bennett, T. (2017). *Creating a culture: How school leaders can optimise behaviour*. CrownCopyright.

Bessant, J., Farthing, R., & Watts, R. (2017). *The precarious generation: A political economy of young people*. Routledge.

Biddulph, S. (1984). *The secret of happy children: A new guide for parents*. Bay Books.

Biddulph, S. (1997). *Raising boys: Why boys are different and how to help them become happy and well-balanced men*. Finch Publishing.

Blackmore, J., & Lauder, H. (2006). Researching policy. In B. Somekh & C. Lewin (Eds.), *Research methods in the social sciences* (pp. 97–105). Sage.

Carpenter, A. (2003, July 1). *Huge improvement in student suspensions* [Media release]. Western Australia Government.

Commissioner for Children and Young People. (2019). *Improving the odds for WA's vulnerable children and young people*.

Committee of Inquiry into Education in Western Australia. (1984). *Education in Western Australia: Report of the Committee of Inquiry appointed by the Minister for Education in Western Australia*. Government Printer.

Connell, R. W., Ashenden, S., Kessler, S., & Dowsett, G. (1982). *Making the difference: Schools, families and social division*. Allen & Unwin.

de Jong, T. (2005). A framework of principles and best practice for managing student behaviour in the Australian education context. *School Psychology International*, 26(3), 353–370.

Ecclestone, K. (2017). Behaviour change policy agendas for "vulnerable" subjectivities: The dangers of therapeutic governance and its new entrepreneurs. *Journal of Education Policy*, 32(1), 48–62.

Education Workforce Initiatives Ministerial Taskforce. (2007). *Education Workforce Initiatives: Report: "If you think education is expensive."*

Fogelgarn, R., & Lewis, R. (2015). "Are you being your best?" Why students behave responsibly. *Australian Journal of Education*, 59(3), 278–292.

Foley, D. (2002). Critical ethnography: The reflexive turn. *Qualitative Studies in Education*, 15(5), 469–490.

Foucault, M. (1979). *Discipline and punish: The birth of the prison* (A. Sheridan, Trans.). Peregrine. (Original work published 1975).

Freire, P. (2004). *Pedagogy of indignation*. Paradigm Publishers.

Frydenberg, E., Ainley, M., & Russell, V. (2005). *Student motivation and engagement* (Schooling Issues Digest 2005/2). Department of Education, Science and Training.

Fullan, M. (1983). *The meaning of educational change.* Teachers' College Press.

Gillies, V. (2016). *Pushed to the edge: Inclusion and behaviour support in schools.* Policy Press.

Giroux, H. (1983). *Theory and resistance in education: A pedagogy for the opposition.* Bergin & Garvey.

Giroux, H. (2023, April 11). Fascist politics in the age of neoliberal capitalism: Confronting the domestication of the unimaginable. *Counterpunch.* https://www.counterpunch.org/2023/04/11/fascist-politics-in-the-age-of-neoliberal-capitalismconfronting-the-domestication-of-the-unimaginable/

Glasser, W. (1969). *Schools without failure.* Harper and Row.

Glasser, W. (1975). *Reality therapy: A new approach to psychiatry.* Perennial Library.

Groundwater-Smith, S., Brennan, M., McFadden, M., & Mitchell, J. (2003). *Secondary schooling in a changing world.* Thomson.

Harber, C. (2004). *Schooling as violence: How schools harm pupils and societies.* RoutledgeFalmer.

Hiatt, B. (2009, January 16). State schools get extra help for disruptive pupils. *The West Australian,* 19.

Hjörne, E., & Säljö, R. (2006). "There is something about Julia"—Symptoms, categories, and the process of invoking ADHD in the Swedish school: A case study. In H. Laude, P. Brown, J. Dillabough, & A. H. Halsey (Eds.), *Education, globalization & social change* (pp. 602–616). Oxford University Press.

House of Representatives, Standing Committee on Employment Education and Training. (1996). *Truancy and exclusion from school: Report of the inquiry into truancy and exclusion of children and young people from school.* Commonwealth Parliament.

Hunter, I. (1994). *Rethinking the school: Subjectivity, bureaucracy, criticism.* Allen & Unwin.

Hunter, M., & Russell, D. (1990). *Mastering coaching and supervision.* Corwin Press.

Hyde, N. (1992). Discipline in Western Australian government schools. In R. Slee (Ed.), *Discipline in Australian public education: Changing policy and practice* (pp. 61–78). Australian Council for Educational Research.

Ingram, E. (2020). *How the education sectors resource and react to student health and wellbeing issues in Western Australia.* https://www.ccyp.wa.gov.au/media/4383/report-how-the-education-sectors-resource-and-react-to-student-health-and-wellbeing-issues-in-western-australia-march-2020.pdf

La Boétie, E. de (1975). *The politics of obedience: The discourse of voluntary servitude* (Harry Kurz, Trans.). Black Rose Books.

Lillico, I. (2000). *Boys & their schooling: A guide for parents and teachers.* Ian Lillico.

Lillico, I. (2001). *Australian issues in boys' education.* Tranton Enterprises.

Lovat, T. (2004). Reading the fine print: Tracking social movements through curriculum analysis. In J. Allen (Ed.), *Sociology of education: Possibilities and practices* (3rd ed., pp. 104–122). Social Science Press.

Luke, C. (1989). *Pedagogy, printing, and protestantism: The discourse on childhood.* State University of New York Press.

Manolev, J., Sullivan, A., & Slee, R. (2019). The datafication of discipline: ClassDojo, surveillance and a performative classroom culture. *Learning, Media and Technology*, 4(1), 36–51.
McDonald, T. (2010). *Classroom management*. Oxford University Press.
McDonald, T. (2019). *Classroom management* (3rd ed.). Oxford University Press.
Meredyth, D., & Tyler, D. (1993). Introduction. In D. Meredyth & D. Tyler (Eds.), *Child and citizen: Genealogies of schooling and subjectivity* (pp. 1–10). Institute for Cultural Studies, Griffin University.
Millei, Z., Griffiths, T., & Parkes, R. (2010). Opening the field: Deliberating over discipline. In Z. Millei, T. Griffiths, & R. Parks (Eds.), *Re-theorizing discipline in education: Problems, politics & possibilities* (pp. 1–12). Peter Lang.
Miller, A. (1990). *For your own good: Hidden cruelty in child-rearing and the roots of violence* (3rd ed.). Noonday Press.
Moore, B. (Ed.). (2004). *The Australian concise Oxford dictionary* (4th ed.). Oxford University Press.
Murphy, C. (2014). *Behaviour management in schools*. Office of the Auditor General Western Australia.
OECD. (2023). *Education policy outlook in Australia* (OECD Education Policy Perspectives, No. 67). OECD Publishing.
Olssen, M. (1999). *Michel Foucault: Materialism and education*. Bergin & Garvey.
Preston, N., & Symes, C. (1992). *Schools and classrooms: A cultural studies analysis of education*. Longman Cheshire.
Rose, N. (1990). *Governing the soul: The shaping of the private self*. Routledge.
Saul, J. (2006). *The collapse of globalism: And the reinvention of the world*. Penguin Books.
Senate, Education and Employment References Committee. (2023). *The issue of increasing disruption in Australian school classrooms: Interim report*. Commonwealth of Australia.
Senate, Education and Employment References Committee. (2024). *The issue of increasing disruption in Australian school classrooms: Final report*. Commonwealth of Australia.
Serres, M., & Latour, B. (1995). *Conversations on science, culture, and time*. Ann Arbor: University of Michigan Press.
Slee, R. (1995). *Changing theories and practices of discipline*. Falmer Press.
Slee, R. (2011). *The irregular school: Exclusion, schooling, and inclusive education*. Routledge.
Slee, R. (2016). Goodbye Mr Chips, hello Dr Phil? In A. Sullivan, B. Johnson, & B. Lucas (Eds.), *Challenging dominant views on student behaviour at school: Answering back* (pp. 63–76). Springer.
Slee, R. (2018). Why I teach. *Idiom*, 54(2), 6–8.
Smith, B. (1991). *Governing classrooms: Privatisation and discipline in Australian schooling* [Ph.D. thesis]. Griffith University.
Tait, G. (2013). *Making sense of mass education*. Cambridge University Press.
Tamboukou, M. (1999). Writing genealogies: An exploration of Foucault's strategies for doing research. *Discourse: Studies in the Cultural Politics of Education*, 20(2), 201–217.
Tamboukou, M. (2016). Education as action/the adventure of education: Thinking with Arendt and Whitehead. *Journal of Educational Administration and History*, 48(2), 136–147.
Taylor, E., & Kearney, A. (2018). School discipline and surveillance: Developments in Australia and Aotearoa/New Zealand. In J. Deakin, E. Taylor, & A. Kupchik (Eds.), *The Palgrave*

international handbook of school discipline, surveillance, and social control (pp. 87–104). Palgrave Macmillan.
Theobald, M. (1990). Introduction. In M. R. Theobald & R. J. W. Selleck (Eds.), *Family, school & state in Australian history* (pp. ix–viv). Allen & Unwin.
Usher, R., & Edwards, R. (1994). *Postmodernism and education*. Routledge.
Vick, M. (2004). Watching the clock: Changes and continuities in schools and society. In J. Allen (Ed.), *Sociology of education: Possibilities and practices* (3rd ed., pp. 54–80). Social Science Press.
WA Department of Education (WADE). (2015a). *Annual report 2014–15*.
WA Department of Education (WADE). (2015b). *Strategic plan for WA Public Schools (2016–2019)*.
WA Department of Education (WADE). (2016). *Annual report 2015–2016*.
WA Department of Education (WADE). (2022). *Annual report 2021–2022*.
WA Department of Education (WADE). (2023). *Engagement centres*. https://www.education.wa.edu.au/-/engagement-centres
WA Department of Education and Training (WADET). (2001). *Behaviour management in schools*.
WA Department of Education and Training (WADET). (2007, August 27). *School suspensions and exclusions under the spotlight* [Media release].
WA Department of Education and Training (WADET). (2008a). *Behaviour management in schools*.
WA Department of Education and Training (WADET). (2008b). *School improvement and accountability framework*.
WA Department of Education and Training (WADET). (2008c, March 16). *Schools crackdown on bad behaviour* [Media release].
WA Department of Education and Training (WADET). (2010, May 21). *Suspensions increase as tough stance on bad behaviour continues* [Media release].
WA Education Department (WAED). (1959). Discipline in the secondary school and classroom. *Education Circular, 61*(1), 20–29.
WA Education Department (WAED). (1972). *Discipline in secondary schools in Western Australia: Report of the Committee of Inquiry chaired by H. W. Dettman*.
WA Education Department (WAED). (1985). *Disruptive behaviour in schools: Report of the Ministerial Working Party chaired by L. W. Louden*.
WA Education Department (WAED). (1995). *Strategic plan 1996–1998*.
WA Education Department (WAED). (1997). *Strategic plan for government schools education 1998–2000*.
WA Education Department (WAED). (1998a). *Behaviour management in schools policy*.
WA Education Department (WAED). (1998b). *Making the difference: Policy and guidelines for students at educational risk*.
WA Education Department (WAED), & Caring School Environment Committee (CSEC). (1982). *The provision of caring environments in secondary schools*. Education Department of Western Australia.

Weaver, J., & Morris, M. (2022). Michel Serres: A pedagogical life. *Educational Philosophy and Theory, 54*(4), 350–352. https://doi.org/10.1080/00131857.2021.1917368

Wright, K. (2010, November–December). *"To see through Johnny and to see Johnny through": The guidance movement in interwar Australia* [Paper presentation]. AARE Conference, Melbourne.

Wright, K. (2014), Student wellbeing and the therapeutic turn in education. *Australian Educational and Developmental Psychologist, 31*(2), 141–152.

· 4 ·

HERON HIGH: CASE STUDY ONE

Introduction

In the tradition of the critical storyteller, this chapter continues to inform the main purpose of this book, to critique school behavior and discipline policies within neoliberal times. By embedding the theory within the text (Apple, 2000, p. 6) of this particular ethnographic case study, I endeavor to get "up close" to the ways in which discipline operates on individual lives. In this task, I draw on my own personal-professional biography of key events, initiatives, incidents, and strategies enacted at a large government secondary school in Western Australia. As Connell (2013) argues, "education itself has a resilience, has a grounding in social needs that cannot be suppressed and that will be heard" (p. 110). Like Connell, I want my story to "be heard" in the hope that it will shed light on the limitations of behaviorist approaches to school discipline with a view to creating a more humane and socially just response to student disaffection. This chapter is based on research conducted at Heron High as part of a Master of Education research project (Robinson, 2005) which was granted university ethics approval. Pseudonyms have been used for all participants and their school throughout this chapter to continue to protect their privacy and confidentiality.

The chapter is organized around three moves. Firstly, I explain my choice of critical ethnography and why it is helpful; secondly, I provide an overview of Heron High School with a focus on its various strategies to manage "problem students" including the School Development Plan, school review, RYPPLE (Raising Young People in Positive Learning Environments), SIS (Student Information Systems), and MTIS (Multi-Tiered Implementation Support); and finally, I identify three emergent themes, namely, the impact of marketization on schools and those who inhabit them; the limitations of "get tough" or "zero tolerance" approaches to school discipline policies, and lastly, the influence of Positive Behavior Schools on discipline policies and practices.

Critical Ethnography and Case Studies

> Essentially, ethnography is a methodology which entails "being there" as an ethnographer in "the field" among "the people" under study with the ambition of understanding and theorizing the meaning of lived experience. (Trondman et al., 2018, p. 31)

In Chapter 1, I briefly explained the foundations of critical ethnography. To reiterate, as a *critical* ethnographer, I have a strong commitment to being there in the field of practice (Foley, 2002). In addition, I aim to develop rapport and trust and do not accept "marginalization as either inevitable nor dependent on the faults of the marginalized and oppressed people themselves" (Beach & Vigo-Arrazola, 2021, pp. 679–680). As Mac an Ghaill and Hayward (2021) explain, a major advantage of critical ethnography is that it enables us to "drill down," opening the field to enable us to ask new questions (p. 463).

In this chapter I endeavor to "drill down" by examining the enactment of school discipline policies at Heron High as both a teacher and apprentice ethnographer (Lave, 2019, p. 4) between the years 1995 and 2005. During this period, Heron High was battling with a range of school improvement reforms and consequently struggled with many accompanying policies including the school's own behavior and discipline policies.

Significant genealogical patterns and neoliberal tectonic shifts, outlined in the previous chapter, influenced my collection of the anecdotal and ethnographic data that will be shared in this chapter. My focus is on comprehending the everyday reality of what has occurred, and continues to occur, for many teachers, families, and young people. This process involves maintaining what Theriault and Mercier (2023) describe as "ethnographic vigilance," which means one cannot remain neutral when confronted with ethical dilemmas "imbued with neoliberal technologies" (p. 17). As Zinn (2022) argues, "you can't be neutral on a moving train," and "education becomes most rich and alive when it confronts the reality of moral conflict in the world" (p. 120).

Case Study One: Heron High

> Policies in practice do not exist and are not enacted in schools separately from one another, despite the tendency for most educational research to treat them as though they do. (Ball et al., 2011, p. 1)

Context

When returning to secondary teaching in Australia, after having lived abroad for five years, I was oblivious to the changes that had occurred within the government public education system I had returned to work within. Prior to this, I had taught for twenty years for this department and assumed it was going to be a "walk in the park." It was only retrospectively that I began to understand how naïve I was. Ball (2021) explains:

> The changes in education and education policy since 1976 have been profound—epistemic even [...] to say, they represent a fundamental shift in organising principles, from welfare education, based on the principles of public service, to neoliberal education, based on the principles of market exchange and competition. (p. 2)

The overcrowded public secondary school I returned to was struggling with these neoliberal devolutionary changes and felt totally unfamiliar to me. This was Heron High in the year 1995. The school was also physically worse for wear (having been built in the 1950s for 400 students) and had expanded to accommodate 1200 by the time I arrived. The region was growing rapidly and no longer dominantly rural and agricultural, nor dependent on timber production, but instead an expanding tourism industry plus attracting many new residents from the city for a lifestyle change. In contrast, a significant number of the students attending the school were the children of single parent and working-class families, many of whom were living on the edge of poverty. Smyth and Wrigley (2013) explain that "school ethos involves creating a climate in which students see adults as supportive, and in which plentiful opportunities exist for students to develop an attachment to the school" (p. 156). The widespread structural reforms occurring within public education at the time, especially the focus on school improvement, self-management, and marketing, resulted in Heron High struggling to find collective ways to work together and cope with these drastic changes and challenges.

School Effectiveness/School Improvement/School Development

As well as the demographic and socio-economic changes I noticed at Heron High on my return to teaching in 1995, I began documenting the impact the school effectiveness and school improvement movement was having on our work as teachers through the critical lens of my Master of Education research (Robinson, 2005). I then began to understand that it was not just our school that was struggling, but many others around the world also part of the global education industry (Thrupp, 2001, p. 30) under attack from economic rationalism (Down, 1994, p. 54), including schools in the United Kingdom, New Zealand, Western Europe, and the United States.

In Australia, leading advocates of this reform, Caldwell and Spinks (1988), published *The self-managing school*. A year later, the Ministry of Education in Western Australia launched *School development plans: Policy and guidelines* (1989), declaring that "the process of devolution required schools be accountable [...] and [...] their planning would help teachers work more effectively and efficiently" (p. 2). Cuttance (1997) agreed that quality assurance required the adoption of "strategic school objectives, regular monitoring of students and an annual review of progress" (p. 105). Heron High was forced to focus on the performance of both teachers and students, and yet these self-managing systems did not improve student learning, "promote teacher professionalism or democratic community practices" (Blackmore, 2002, p. 39) and, even worse, failed those students most in need.

At Heron High, the School Development Plan (SDP) was closely linked to an enforced K-12 curriculum framework. In 2003, the school changed its priority within the SDP because of the Western Australian Education Department's new Strategic Plan 2003–2006, later to become the Plan for Government Schools 2004–2007 (WADET, 2003a). The priority was "to improve the outcomes of all pupils" (WADET, 2003a, p. 1), placing greater emphasis on student academic performance, which was to be measured using the government's newly released "standards" (WADET, 2003b).

This reform meant that schools like Heron High were not only more accountable for student performance (Gleeson & Gunter, 2001, p. 140), but at the same time dialogic spaces for teachers were dismantled (Shacklock & Smyth, 1997, p. 16). This occurred in the context of "pursuing image and impression management strategies (for example, through advertising, school uniforms, and discipline policy" (Smyth, 2001b, p. 25).

The Behavior Management and Discipline Strategy

In 2001, all public schools in Western Australia were required to have their own behavior management plan to implement the Behavior Management in Schools policy guidelines. Heron High was one of the first secondary schools to qualify for the newly introduced behavior management strategy (WADE, 2001) based on a combination of the ranking of socio-economic census data (known as the "H" index); the number of suspensions and exclusions; school attendance; workers' compensation claims attributed to student behavior; and the level of juvenile offences in the region.

Heron's "H" index at this time was the third lowest in Western Australia, which meant the school was allocated discretionary funds (Azad, 2008) to be spent on professional development in "behavior management." Heron High's choice, like many other government schools throughout Western Australia during this period, was to employ Canadian consultants Barrie Bennett and Peter Smilanich's CMS (classroom management skills) that were packaged with accompanying influential textbooks, manuals, and workshops. Their CMS program (Bennett & Smilanich, 1994) was also promoted and partly financed by the Western Australian State School Teachers' Union.

During the following years, the situation did not improve for the students regardless of investments in consultants and intensive skills training for teachers. The series of incidents that followed included an increase in rebellious behaviors by many students and a deterioration of classroom relationships as students were continually monitored on their compliance with "codes of conduct" alongside their academic performance. This led to many teachers, including myself, being monitored, observed, and scrutinized to see how efficiently we were implementing the CMS training in our classrooms. Maguire et al. (2010) explain that these formal technical and instructional systems "through which the school imposes and maintains its view of order" (p. 153) can be used to signal a failure of the teacher's management, "an inability to teach or that the school itself is 'failing'" (p. 154).

While the Behavior Management and Discipline Strategy (BMaD) was "intended to increase the competence and confidence of teachers to support and engage students" (Robson et al., 2008, p. v), it resulted in greater divisions between learning areas, segregation between administration and teaching staff, and a culture of competition for limited resources and positions of power. I described this form of "balkanization" (Hargreaves, 1994) in the following journal entry.

> Every Monday morning the chime calls us into the staff room for our weekly briefings. We wander down the corridors in our subject hubs. (I call them clans.) Some "clans" are checking that others are not too early. It is against union directives. We assemble at our respective tables and the late ones hang at the door. The same ritual happens at after-school staff meetings. There is a silence as we await to hear the briefings. I often catch myself changing mood from one of rested, jovial, and optimistic after the weekend to one of somber sadness and I witness the same vein surround as the focus is on keeping discipline and control. This, I suddenly realize, is what it is to be oppressed. We *have to* be there; we *must* listen to *how we need* to behave in our teaching style. What a way to begin each week! Reports of who has been suspended for non-compliance, who to send to the front office if they turn up, which reports, papers, meetings must be attended to. How we must not let students out of class. How the yard duty roster is being reinforced. Who needs to volunteer for what. Who needs to rove to maintain order. My head starts spinning. There is no discussion nor debate. Only orders. I look around and see the same blank faces that reflect what I am feeling. We all must go and teach in five minutes and I fear our students are going to be infected with the same morose mood. (Teaching journal, June 2003)

These centrally imposed policies (Maguire et al., 2010) leave "very little wriggle-room" for teachers because "formally coded sets of discipline policies have to be seen as responsive and compliant" (p. 165). These policies and accompanying codes of conduct make no attempt to challenge nor address inequitable power structures and practices that have contributed to social exclusion and educational disadvantage and therefore "little wriggle-room" to genuinely engage with students.

Pink Slips and Wellbeing

My journal and ethnographic field notes provided additional insight into the seemingly innocuous practices arising out of punitive discipline policies, for example: "This week we are targeting getting to class on time, therefore please issue pink slips and demerit points for non-complaint behavior to keep the clientele on task" (Field notes, Monday morning briefing August 2003).

No matter what the rules or incentives (no matter how detailed or well monitored) they will be insufficient to address complex pedagogical problems in the ways envisaged by those in charge (Schwartz & Sharpe, 2010, p. 5). The second example of this relates to a teaching staff health and wellbeing survey conducted by the administration a few months later, which revealed that all was not well. There were reports of staff bullying and concerns about disruptive students. The survey was used to deliver some key messages:

- Message 1: Teachers' workload has increased due to an increasing requirement to manage disruptive students.
- Message 3: Staff get lots of their positive reward from good kids doing a good job.
- Message 4: Management of difficult disruptive students is a big issue.
- Message 8: There is a significant staff bullying issue (Staff survey results, November 2003).

My teaching journal at the beginning of the following year reinforced the extent to which relationships deteriorated as the school hunkered down with a "get tough" approach to student behavior.

Professional Assault Response Training

Day one and we are back at it again. I limped in, literally, not sure whether my feelings of apathy and disillusionment would give me away. I had decided this year to take a very low profile and instead seek out glimmers of hope that shine through the cracks occasionally. Well, I did not last long. The speaker for the day was giving us a spiel on "Verbal Judo." His body language already had me offside. His language included clichés and condescending comments [...] "having your heart in teaching," using "peace phrases," "don't be a dinosaur and accept change." (I was already agitated.) He then told us that we were there to spend a day with him to learn "tactics" that enable us to redirect hostility and defuse danger. It was for our own safety and protection! He was from the tactical training unit of the police service. Thoughts flashed through my mind of the schools in America that had recently employed police to patrol their corridors as a method of discipline. Is that where we head next? What has this to do with teaching? When he then informed us that, as professionals, our main goal in our work was to aim for voluntary compliance and eliminate any "why" questioning, I was sure again that I was in the wrong environment. I looked around the crowded hall at the other 100 returning school staff attending this compulsory day of "professional development." They appeared to be passively sitting, listening, occasionally nodding. At the first chance, I left the hall in a dizzy state and took myself away to my desk and did some preparation for the new teaching term. I stayed alone for the rest of the day. A few days later, I was in trouble because my absence had been noted. (Teaching journal, January 2004)

At heart, my experience of feeling "on the outer" reflected my unease at the implementation of what Saltman (2014, p. 43) calls "grit," or a pedagogy of control and rule following, plus my low status in the school's hierarchy (Hargreaves 1994, p. 215) as the behavior management policy was being "interpreted and enacted" (Maguire et al., 2010, p. 167).

Uniforms and SIS

By 2006, the Western Australian Minister for Education directed all government schools to adopt school uniforms, apparently to improve student safety and behavior, and then in 2007 a further directive was given by the Minister that denim be removed from school uniforms (WADET, 2007). Heron High had already been trialing the school uniform policy in the mid-1990s, firstly with a simple silk-screened branded t-shirt then a decade later, a more formal polo shirt embossed and endorsed with the school coat of arms.

During this time, the compulsory school uniform became the cause of many discipline struggles and behavior infringements, especially for those students who were living in dire family situations (including unemployment, domestic violence, drug and alcohol abuse, incarceration, and severe mental health issues). In contrast, another decade later, when parents throughout the state public schooling system started to complain about the costs of having their child in a compulsory uniform, the then Minister for Education stated that "students coming to school smartly dressed in shirts and ties is uplifting for the whole community and should be applauded" (Hiatt, 2016, p. 26).

2006 was also the year that the Student Information System (SIS) software was activated at Heron High for the purpose of school reports and recording of behavior management incidents. Not being in full school uniform was considered an infringement of the code of conduct.

The 10 Point Action Plan

Matters did not improve regarding the learning environment of many students and teachers attending government secondary schools, including Heron High. "Schools get tough" (Mercer, 2018); "Escalating violence in WA schools prompts serious policy review" (Barry, 2018): these were two of many headlines and opinion articles featured in the media in July of 2018 after serious physical altercations had occurred in public schools in Western Australia. The education minister (Ellery, 2018) stated: "we're drawing a line in the sand" and an "action plan will be released by the Department of Education for public schools, considered and agreed on by all stakeholders" (p. 18).

The education minister launched the "anti-violence in schools 10-point Action Plan" (WADE, 2018), to be implemented at the beginning of the 2019 school year including "automatic suspensions of up to 10 days for students who attack others or start fights" (Hiatt, 2019b). Action 6 of the plan required further changes to the school's practices in that "every school must add 'Good Standing' requirements to its behaviour policy" and "those students who do the wrong thing will have privileges removed" and only "earn back 'Good Standing' by making amends and behaving well" (WADE, 2018). The "getting tough" attitude did not help the situation, even after community forums, hosted by Heron High in June 2018, attempted to reassure parents that positive behavior and values such as respect and empathy were going to be taught explicitly. This situation was not unique to Heron High. The following year Hiatt (2019a) reported "almost 1,000 students have been suspended from Western Australian public schools for physical aggression in the first four weeks of the school year—a 15 per cent increase on the same time last year." Yet the same media article (Hiatt, 2019a) stated that "Education Minister Sue Ellery said the figures showed the McGowan Government's crackdown on school violence was working."

This type of "getting tough" "action plan" to exclude disruptive students from schools without any understanding of the complexity of the causes of violence, anger, and aggression, and the cultural, political, economic, and social issues underlying them has time and time again been proven ineffectual (see, e.g., Miller, 1990; Osler & Starkey, 2005; Slee, 1995).

Positive Behavior RYPPLE (Raising Young People in Positive Learning Environments)

In 2019, Heron High, like many other schools struggling with behavior management reforms, adopted Positive Behavior systems such as RYPPLE (Raising Young People in Positive Learning Environments). Leading staff were invited by "world leader" and American Dr. Tim Lewis, from the University of the Missouri Center for Positive Behavior, to present at the Chicago Leadership Forum on Positive Behavior Interventions and Supports. This was followed by these schools hosting summits on "Changing Classroom Behaviour: Systems to Support Effective Classroom Practice" led by Tim Lewis and visiting associates, focusing on emotional and behavioral disorders. By 2022 Heron High, like other schools, announced that they were a Positive Behavior Support (PBS) school that taught the values of Respect, Empathy, Achievement and Learning (REAL).

The following year, another RYPPLE summit was held, again led by Tim Lewis, for participants and their schools to learn how to collect, use, and analyze student data for problem solving and assessment information. Positive learning regimes like RYPPLE are not only alive and well at Heron High and its feeder primary schools but continue to spread globally. In Australia, for example, this organization is registered as a charity with the Australian Charities and Not-for-Profits Commission, claiming "to increase student engagement and social and behavioural success" (RYPPLE, 2023).

MTIS (Multi-Tiered Implementation Support)

As well as positive learning, a Multi-Tiered Implementation Support (MTIS) model was adopted by many high schools, including Heron High "as a systematic, targeted, and efficient approach to teacher professional learning to increase their implementation of classroom management and instructional practices" (Telfer, 2020, p. 167). This model aligned with the Senate Education and Employment References Committee's (2023) interim report *The issue of increasing disruption in Australian school classrooms* which:

> Recommends that Education Ministers, as part of the next National School Reform Agreement, require evidence-based instructional models, such as *explicit instruction; formative assessment; mastery learning; and spacing and retrieval*, which have been proven effective at creating a learning climate that manages disruptive behaviour in classrooms and provides the best possible learning conditions, to be implemented. (p. iv, emphasis added)

These recommendations also aligned with the most recent Western Australian Student Behavior in Public Schools Policy (WADE, 2023), which included an increased emphasis on "positivist behaviour, including students recognising and regulating their own emotions," "build[ing] staff capability through training," plus "a multi-tiered approach being adopted by the school."

In the next section, I draw together three dominant themes that have emerged from this case study. These three themes are: (i) marketization of public education policy; (ii) getting tough on kids and zero tolerance and (iii) the growth of positive behavior support (PBS).

Key Themes

Theme One: Marketization of Public Education Policy

> Politicians, businessmen including management consultants, measurement experts, economists and education system managers now form the arena in which education policy is made. (Connell, 2015, p. 193)

In the first section of this chapter, I shared my experiences of returning to a large public secondary school that was implementing versions of the school improvement and school effectiveness reform movement. I noticed the impact it was having, not only on me personally, but also my colleagues and the children that I taught. The school was being "pushed and shoved towards an impersonal homogeneity" (Angus, 2012, p. 245). This felt unfamiliar, even though I had two decades of professional teaching experience behind me. The new behavior management industry was an alien concept for me. I was concerned about the ways in which "a commitment to the public good" (Thompson, 2020, p. 4) was being subverted by "technocratic acts" (van Manen, 2002, p. 32) centrally driven and enforced at the school level (Maguire et al., 2010, p. 165).

At Heron High, like many other schools, agendas and plans were swirling around every corner, every space, every meeting, every encounter: "school development," "school improvement," "strategic plans," "standards," "outcomes," and "performance indicators." The school also employed a range of consultants to advise on how to plan and improve the school to reach these benchmarks. These were often advisors from the corporate world, many of whom had never been involved in education. As teachers experiencing the effects of neoliberal reform, we found ourselves trapped in a cycle of data collection and review to ensure that the school was fitting within the boundaries of a regulated, top-down accountability system. This included regular audits held by the District Office, the checking of our results to use as "data," and ensuring that average grades were good enough for the "increasingly muscular forms of inspection and appraisal" (Smyth, 2001a, p. 168). In turn, whilst we experienced this kind of deskilling and de-professionalization of teachers' work, we also experienced the pressure placed upon students to conform and comply with rules and regulations that aligned with the goals of improving standards within an "audit culture" (Power, 1999).

A major consequence of this performance culture was an increasing emphasis on streaming students into academic or non-academic pathways. Academic students were identified by their test results both in primary and middle school on math, literacy, and science, while those deemed to be non-academic were cajoled and guided into vocational education and training courses more suited to their interests and abilities. As a practical arts teacher, I was no longer considered "experienced" as I was required to be "upskilled" with certified competency-based training. This involved little new professional learning in my field but, instead, focused on checking and ticking boxes (key performance indicators) and "gathering" evidence. As Apple (2000) explains, what I was experiencing, together with many of my colleagues, was the loss of control over our "own labor" (p. 116). We had to forfeit our "autonomous teaching methods, chosen texts, modes of assessments and learning outcomes" (Apple, 2000, p. 116), leaving limited possibility of engaging in peer teaching and healthy interactions with one another. Reid (1999) observes that, "as the identity of teachers shifts from one of common membership of a profession, to that of individual operating in an education market, so too, do the prospects for solidarity and collective action decline" (p. 197).

In the context of the marketization of public schooling, Heron High, like many public secondary schools, focused on their corporate image in a competitive market: what dress standards were required (of both staff and students), what billboard information and advertising would be used, and how to talk to the local media. For a short period, Heron High even signed up to a sponsorship/fundraising campaign matched with students selling vouchers for a new information technology laboratory. Fielding and Moss (2011) explain how these market forces permeate the culture of schooling:

> A combination of economism and techno-bureaucratism has enveloped education [...] we are left with an enfeebled democracy practising a pseudo-politics and occupying a contracting public sphere; infused with a certain form of economic thinking and reduced to arguing differences of detail about technical and managerial matters; and subjected to an array of experts, consultants and entrepreneurs, who both build and assess the effectiveness of an increasing array of human technologies that are used to govern us ever more effectively. (p. 21)

Theme Two: Getting Tough on Kids and Zero Tolerance

Given the pressures to "improve" under market and managerialist reform, a culture of control and compliance soon permeates school discipline policies in schools like Heron High. This results in more stringent rules for everyone; and greater surveillance of those who do not meet the deadlines, reach the benchmarks, or comply with the image. Under a regime of "clamping down," some students were singled out as being "at risk" and infringements were recorded permanently on the Student Information System (SIS). This was followed by loss of "privileges" such as school excursions or end of year events, all resulting in those students who most needed help not feeling confident to safely come forward, thus complex problems remained "underground, further threatening self, family, school, and community" (Fine & Smith, 2001, p. 258). Many of these students were also placed on "Individual Behavior Plans" and monitored each lesson, each day. This loss of freedom, combined with a loss of "democratic right," spilled out into fights and an escalation of violence, which in turn was sensationalized by the media. A "10 point anti-violence action plan" (WADE, 2018) was then introduced by the Minister of Education and resulted in a further increase in student suspensions as stated in the Education Departments' annual report (WADE, 2022):

> Since the launch in late 2018 of Let's take a stand together, the state government's plan to address violence in schools, the numbers of students suspended and excluded have increased. In 2021, 18,068 students (5.5% of total enrolments throughout the year) were suspended compared to 15,943 in 2020 (4.9%). There were 76 students excluded in 2021, 72 students in 2020 and 65 in 2019 compared to 24 in 2018 and 8 in each of 2017 and 2016. (p. 29)

Theme Three: The Growth of Positive Behavior Support (PBS)

When the media reported unruly behavior in Western Australian schools (Hiatt, 2013), one academic expert blamed "the children's bad wiring in their brains and neuroscience instead would help students to learn how to regulate their own emotions" (as cited in Hiatt, 2013). This pathologization of behavior, or "deficit thinking," "locates the responsibility in the lived experiences of children [. . .] rather than locating responsibility within classroom interactions, relationships, and the education system" (Shields et al., 2005, p. xx).

Many students who do not conform, comply, meet the education standards, nor engage in their learning are often labeled "at risk" and "disorderly," and become "collateral damage" (Bauman, 2011), to be dismissed as in need of therapy because of emotional and behavior disorders. Heron High, like many other public schools, became a "Positive Behavior Support" (PBS) school, accompanied by the REAL (Respect, Empathy, Achievement and Learning) award program, explicitly teaching values as a potential solution. In these schools, the focus is on emotional intelligence, and on frameworks of stepped self-control, self-discipline, and self-regulation, and teachers are trained to adopt tactical tools and strategies at workshops and seminars. PBS, also known as School-Wide Positive Behavior Support and often accompanied by Multi-Tiered Implementation Support (MTIS) systems, has been promoted and reviewed by organizations and researchers such as RYPPLE (2023), Victoria Department of Education (2020), Subban et al. (2020), and Leif et al. (2021). Maguire et al. (2010), a decade earlier, had already investigated the promotion and promises of these fashionable theoretical and pedagogical approaches which were saturating the English secondary system at the time and based on the promise of "solv[ing] any student disruption in school" (p. 154). In their words: "sets of procedures are advocated that have to be followed systematically in the classroom, and through a consistent whole-school approach, in order to ensure student compliance, managed through stepped sets of rewards and sanctions" (p. 155).

Maguire et al. (2010) found that these positive behavior models had failed in their mission because they had predominately considered "psychologistic approaches" above and beyond the "sociological" (p. 155). The sociological approach, in contrast to managerial and technical approaches, "question[s] the social and political conditions" of our schools and our work in them (Angus, 1994, p. 81). These questions include:

> What counts as educational practice? What counts as knowledge? Whose interests are served or restricted by the selection, production, distribution and management of such knowledge and practice? What aspects of society and economy are legitimated by forms of schooling? What kind of society do we want? How might schools contribute to the formation of such a society? (Angus, 1994, p. 90)

Conclusion

In this chapter I have shared personal-professional insights and experiences as a teacher and researcher through an in-depth ethnographic case study of one secondary school that I worked in for over a decade. I traced the evolution of a range of strategies used to manage student behavior in the school, including school development and behavior management planning, school reviews, RYPPLE, SIS, and MTIS.

Significant genealogical patterns and tectonic shifts outlined in the previous chapter influenced the collection of this ethnographic data, which I then summarized into three emergent themes: the impact of marketization on schools, the limitations of zero tolerance approaches, and the emergence and influence of Positive Behavior Support (PBS) models.

In the next chapter, I will be sharing in-depth ethnographic field research conducted at another secondary school, as I trace and critique the evolution and enactment of school behavior and discipline policies and practices through the understandings, interpretations, and experiences of the young people I interviewed as part of my Ph.D. research. It is not only my voice as storyteller, but also their voices, that speak back to behavior and discipline discourses. The significant themes collected from both ethnographic sites are then drawn together to share insights that speak directly from the field for further discussion and critique.

References

Angus, L. (1994). Sociological analysis and education management: The social context of the self managing school. *British Journal of Sociology of Education*, 15(1), 79–91.

Angus, L. (2012). Teaching within and against the circle of privilege: Reforming teachers, reforming schools. *Journal of Education Policy*, 27(2), 231–251.

Apple, M. W. (2000). *Official knowledge: Democratic education in a conservative age*. Routledge.

Azad, U. (2008, February 20). McGowan stands up for high school's reputation. *The Mail*, 14.

Ball, S. J. (2021). *The education debate* (4th ed.). Policy Press.

Ball, S., Hoskins, K., Maguire, M., & Braun, A. (2011). Disciplinary texts: A policy analysis of national and local behaviour policies. *Critical Studies in Education*, 52(1), 1–14.

Barry, H. (2018, July 30). Escalating violence in WA schools prompts serious policy review. *WA Today*. https://www.watoday.com.au/national/western-australia/escalating-violence-in-wa-s-schools-prompts-serious-policy-review-20180730-p4zucw.html

Bauman, Z. (2011). *Collateral damage: Social inequalities in a global age*. Polity.

Beach, D., & Vigo-Arrazola, B. (2021). Critical ethnographies of education and for social and educational transformation: A meta-ethnography. *Qualitative Inquiry*, 27(6), 677–688.

Bennett, B., & Smilanich, P. (1994). *Classroom management: A thinking & caring approach*. Bookation.

Blackmore, J. (2002). Restructuring public schooling: A commentary on the New South Wales proposal "Building the Future." *Journal of the HEIA*, 9(1), 37–46.

Caldwell, B., & Spinks, J. (1988). *The self-managing school*. The Falmer Press.

Connell, R. (2013). The neoliberal cascade and education: An essay on the market agenda and its consequences. *Critical Studies in Education*, 54(2), 99–112.

Connell, R. (2015). Markets all around: Defending education in a neoliberal time. In H. Proctor, P. Brownlee, & P. Freebody (Eds.), *Controversies in education: Orthodoxy and heresy in policy and practice* (pp. 181–197). Springer International Publishing. https://doi.org/10.1007/978-3-319-08759-7_16

Cuttance, P. (1997). Quality assurance for schools. In T. Townsend (Ed.), *Restructuring and quality: Ideas for tomorrow's schools* (pp. 100–114). Routledge.

Down, B. (1994). Human capital theory and secondary education. *Unicorn*, 20(3), 54–61.

Ellery, S. (2018, July 30). We're drawing a line in the sand over school violence. *The West Australian*, 18. https://thewest.com.au/opinion/were-drawing-a-line-in-the-sand-over-school-violence-ng-b889110612

Fielding, M., & Moss, P. (2011). *Radical education and the common school: A democratic alternative*. Routledge.

Fine, M., & Smith, K. (2001). Zero tolerance: Reflections on a failed policy that won't die. In W. Ayers, B. Dohn, & R. Ayers (Eds.), *Zero tolerance: Resisting the drive for punishment in our schools: A handbook for parents, students, educators, and citizens* (pp. 256–263). New York Press.

Foley, D. (2002). Critical ethnography: The reflexive turn. *Qualitative Studies in Education*, 15(5), 469–490.

Gleeson, D., & Gunter H. (2001). The performing school and the modernisation of teachers. In D. Gleeson & C. Husbands (Eds.), *The performing school: Managing, teaching and learning in a performance culture* (pp. 140–158). Routledge/Falmer.

Hargreaves, A. (1994). *Changing teachers, changing times: Teachers' work and culture in the Postmodern age*. Cassell.

Hiatt, B. (2013, May 4–5). Lessons in behaviour lacking. *The Weekend West*, 81.

Hiatt, B. (2016, June 11–12). Parents' fury over school uniform costs. *The Weekend West*, 26.

Hiatt, B. (2019a, March 12). Almost 1000 students suspended from WA public schools for physical aggression. *The West Australian*, 5.

Hiatt, B. (2019b, November 16–17). School plan in trouble. *The Weekend West*, 41.

Lave, J. (2019). *Learning and everyday life: Access, participation, and changing practice*. Cambridge University Press. https://doi.org/10.1017/9781108616416

Leif, E., Allen, K., Fox, R., & Stocker, K. (2021). *A review of the evidence for multi-tiered systems of support*. Victorian Department of Education and Training.

Mac an Ghaill, M., & Hayward, C. (2021). Ethnography, methodological autonomy and self-representational space: A reflexive millennial generation of Muslim young men. *Ethnography and Education*, 16(4), 457–474.

Maguire, M., Ball, S., & Braun, A. (2010). Behaviour, classroom management and student "control": Enacting policy in the English secondary school. *International Studies in Sociology of Education*, 20(2), 153–170.

Mercer, D. (2018, July 30). Schools get tough: More kids to be kicked out for violence. *The West Australian*, 1, 9.

Miller, A. (1990). *For your own good: Hidden cruelty in child-rearing and the roots of violence* (3rd ed.). Noonday Press.

Osler, A., & Starkey, H. (2005). Violence in schools and representations of young people: A critique of government policies in France and England. *Oxford Review of Education*, 31(2), 195–215.

Power, M. (1999). *The audit society: Rituals of verification*. Oxford University Press.

Reid, A. (1999). Controlling the curriculum work of teachers. In B. Johnson & A. Reid (Eds.), *Contesting the curriculum* (pp. 186–200). Social Science Press.

Robinson, J. (2005). *A journey in re(claiming) teaching: A critical ethnography of Cape Neal PublHigh School* [Master of Education thesis]. Edith Cowan University.

Robson, G., Angus, M., & McDonald, T. (2008). *An evaluation of the behaviour management & discipline strategy 2001–2007.* Edith Cowan University.

RYPPLE. (2023). *Rypple.* https://rypple.org.au

Saltman, K. J. (2014). The austerity school: Grit, character, and the privatization of public education. *Symploke, 22*(1–2), 41–57.

Schwartz, B., & Sharpe, K. (2010). *Practical wisdom: The right way to do the right thing.* Riverhead.

Senate, Education and Employment References Committee. (2023). *The issue of increasing disruption in Australian school classrooms: Interim report.* Commonwealth of Australia.

Shacklock, G., & Smyth, J. (1997). *Searching for the sine qua non of the collaborative research act* (Occasional paper). School of Education, Finders University.

Shields, C. M., Bishop, R., & Mazawi, A. E. (2005). *Pathologizing practices: The impact of deficit thinking on education.* Peter Lang.

Slee, R. (1995). Pathologies of school violence: A reconsideration. In J. Bessant, K. Carrington, & S. Cook (Eds.), *Cultures of crime and violence: The Australian experience* (pp. 16–23). La Trobe University Press & Victorian Law Foundation.

Smyth, J. (2001a). *Critical politics of teachers work: An Australian perspective.* Peter Lang.

Smyth, J. (2001b, July). *What's happening to teachers' work?* [Lansdowne Lecture]. University of Victoria, British Columbia.

Smyth, J., & Wrigley, T. (2013). *Living on the edge: Rethinking poverty, class and schooling.* Peter Lang.

Subban, P., Sharma, U., Leif, E., & Patnaik, S. (2020). *Five ways to use positive behaviour support strategies in your classroom.* Monash University. https://www.monash.edu/education/teachspace/articles/five-ways-to-use-positive-behaviour-support-strategies-in-your-classroom

Telfer, S. (2020). *Effects of a within-school coaching model on teachers' use of behavioural feedback and opportunities to respond* [Professional Doctorate thesis]. Murdoch University.

Theriault, V., & Mercier, J. (2023). Illustrations of ethical dilemmas during ethnographic fieldwork: When social justice meets neoliberalism in adult education. *Ethnography and Education, 18*(1), 4–20.

Thompson, P. (2020). *School scandals: Blowing the whistle on the corruption of our education system.* Policy Press.

Thrupp, M. (2001). Sociological and political concerns about school effectiveness research: Time for a new research agenda. *School Effectiveness and School Improvement, 12*(1), 7–40.

Trondman, M., Willis, P., & Lund, A. (2018). Lived forms of schooling: Bringing the elementary forms of ethnography to the science of education. In D. Beach, C. Bagley, & S. Marquez da Silva (Eds.), *Handbook of ethnography of education* (pp. 31–49). Wiley.

Van Manen, M. (2002). *The tone of teaching.* Althouse Press.

Victoria Department of Education. (2020). *School-wide positive behaviour support framework.* https://www2.education.vic.gov.au/pal/behaviour-students/guidance/5-school-wide-positive-behaviour-support-swpbs-framework

WA Department of Education (WADE). (2001). *Behaviour management in schools.*

WA Department of Education (WADE). (2018). *Let's take a stand together: Minister's statement on school violence.*

WA Department of Education (WADE). (2022). *Annual report 2021–2022*.

WA Department of Education (WADE). (2023). *Student behaviour in public schools policy version 3.0*.

WA Department of Education and Training (WADET). (2003a). *Plan for government schools 2004–2007*.

WA Department of Education and Training (WADET). (2003b). *Western Australian Government School Standards* (Preview Package).

WA Department of Education and Training (WADET). (2007). *Dress requirements for students in WA public schools*.

Zinn, H. (2022). *You can't be neutral on a moving train: A personal history*. Beacon Press.

· 5 ·

ANCHORAGE HIGH: CASE STUDY TWO

Introduction

Anchorage High is a government (public) secondary school where I conducted research for my Ph.D. 13 years ago (Robinson, 2011). Writing this book affords me an opportunity to revisit this research where I spent considerable time observing, listening, and recording the impact of school behavior and discipline policies on young people because as Welch (2022) argues, "policies always need to be seen in their social and institutional context" (p. 252). The passing of time has not diminished the significance of the issues raised by students back then. On the contrary, they remain as relevant and potent today as when I first heard them. Anchorage has similar demographics to Heron High where I worked as a teacher and researcher (see Chapter 4). My research project at Anchorage (like Heron) was carried out with university ethics approval, and pseudonyms continue to be used to protect the privacy and confidentiality of all participants and their schools.

The students I interviewed at Anchorage were in their third year of high school and their average age was 16. Some of the students had been in primary school together, so had been classmates for at least a decade. These included Jen and Shane, two of the 27 students I had the privilege of speaking with at

Anchorage. As Jen and Shane became more comfortable in my interview with them, they generously shared insight into their personal experiences and more "intimate information" (Russell, 2013, p. 58). In the example below, Jen and Shane discovered they had mutual experiences related to their birth mothers who had spent time in the same prison.

JEN:	I have pictures of my Mum when she was in jail. We have so much in common [talking to Shane].
SHANE:	Yeah, my Mum was in prison for a year—her sentence was for two, but one year was probation [good behavior].
ME:	how was that for you?
SHANE:	Bad, like she was in prison for my birthday, Christmas, and everything.
ME:	What about you, Jen?
JEN:	Yeah, my Mum went various times for a lot of different things.
ME:	How was that for you?
JEN:	I was 6 years old, so I was allowed to stay overnight with her.
SHANE:	Yeah, the same.
JEN:	There were these houses and playgrounds; I think it was Carradale Prison.
SHANE:	Yeah, did it have a fence with no barbwire?
JEN [BECOMING VERY EXCITED]:	YEAH!
SHANE:	That was so good . . . OH MY GOD! our Mums went to the same prison! It had actual little houses, little kitchens.
JEN:	Yeah, they had TV and everything.
SHANE:	They had their own rooms and about four people under one roof. I remember that because we had roast chicken and gravy for tea. (Interview with Jen and Shane, August 2007)

Madison (2005) explains that intimate information of this kind "has consequences" and our interpretation and representation "holds a great deal of power" (p. 4). For me this demands a "politics of positionality" (p. 6), by which I mean a willingness to declare where I stand and in whose interests. My reason for sharing this conversation with Jen and Shane is to draw attention not only to the complexity of young lives but the enormous ethical, educational, and political responsibility we face as critical ethnographers in creating spaces for young people to speak about the things that matter to them.

In the following section, firstly I describe the broader context in which the research was conducted and the ways in which it permeates the lives of the young people interviewed. Secondly, I will discuss some of the challenges of this ethnographic research and how I managed them. Thirdly, the contextual focus shifts to examine four disciplinary strategies: codes of conduct and school exclusion; "Good Standing" and uniform policies; monitoring and surveillance; and warehousing of students.

In the section that follows, I identify and describe two emergent themes: (i) compliance, resistance, and "dropping out"; and (ii) relationships and belonging. Finally, this chapter concludes with three important insights arising from both case study sites, Heron High and Anchorage High. These important and urgent messages provide an opportunity for students to be heard and to speak back to school discipline policies impacting on their lives in neoliberal times (Beach & Vigo-Arrazola, 2021).

Anchorage High

> Ethnography is situated, it is concerned for the mediating effects of specific settings and extended periods of time are spent in these settings. (Youdell, 2006, p. 60)

Context

Anchorage High has similar social, economic, and educational demographics to Heron High, the school that I had previously worked in. Anchorage was also an overcrowded public government school consisting of more than 1,000 students and over 100 teaching staff at the time of my research. Anchorage too was located within a low socio-economic area. The 2021 *Dropping off the edge* report (Tanton et al., 2021) shows that Anchorage remains one of the areas of highest disadvantage in Western Australia, based on "low income; youth not in employment, education or training; and jobless parents" (p. 146). The truancy rate and incidents leading to exclusions from Anchorage were significantly high. Kylie, another of the students I interviewed, explained why:

KYLIE: I have had four behavior cards; when teachers cannot put up with your behavior you get put on a behavior card. They change the color every year, so that you can't copy or forge them.

ME: I don't understand. Why would people want to forge behavior cards?

KYLIE: So they don't get suspended. If they are constantly getting bad behavior reports on their cards, then your rights get taken away, like, your "Good Standing." That means you can't go on excursions and extra-curriculum things and stuff like that. Then the next step is that you get suspended, and the next step is you get expelled. So, the system doesn't really work! (Interview with Kylie, July 2007)

Anchorage, built in the 1970s, like Heron High, was badly in need of repair and, due to overcrowding, had additional demountable or transportable classrooms surrounded by security fencing and locked gates that closely resembled a prison. These gates were only opened for students to be dropped off in the mornings and then exit again at the end of each school day. As an outsider to the school, I was required to sign in and out at the front registry office each time I visited.

Entering the School Gates

In my research plan I intended to invite Year 10 students (16 years of age) to volunteer to be interviewed. I wanted to present my research intentions to the entire student cohort to feel confident that students were welcomed to tell their own story, voluntarily and purposefully (Burgess, 1988). I had planned to interview students who had not been labeled prior to my visit in the binary of "difficult" or "model" students by their teachers and administrators. Both these plans were challenged by the school administrators. For example, during my first meeting with the designated administrator from Anchorage, I was informed that a sample of "troublesome" students had been arranged for me to survey. This sample data set had been collated using the school's "Student Information System" (SIS). In the following extract from my field notes I reveal some of the tensions I faced in recruiting student participants at Anchorage:

> Finally, I am escorted into the DP's office. Introductions and pleasantries abound. He is continually interrupted with incoming calls, forms to be signed, and budget decisions that urgently need endorsement. In between, he does manage to give me a copy of the school's Behavior Management Plan (BMP) and states that the school has received specific funding towards this. He then asked me what I wanted the school to do towards my research project, and offers, on behalf of the administration team, to pick out some "pointy edge kids" for my sample to save me time and effort. I politely decline the offer and explain that I would prefer to speak to and invite *all* Year 10 students. The deputy expresses concern over this decision as he claims that is a too highly ordered task for students and warns there will be much apathy when it comes to dealing with the consent forms. (Field notes, February 2007)

One of the main challenges for me throughout this research was being the outsider. Some of the responses I received, including closed faculty doors and various power dynamics experienced in the staffroom, reminded me of similar staffroom conversations at Heron High. These often comprised disrespectful and derogatory comments about young people as "losers" or "bad," and teachers like myself, questioning these labels, viewed as "not toeing the line," nor "drawing a tough enough line in the sand."

I had chosen to interview Year 10 students (average age 16) because this cohort seemed to clash regularly with behavior management rules. It was also the most homogeneous school group prior to students being streamed into upper secondary school where they were typically divided between academic and vocational pathways. I also found this age group to be mature beyond the expectations or understandings of a school, and often dismissed, because conformity, control, and business as usual too often takes precedence over getting to know these young people and forming genuine relationships with them.

I then presented my research plans and aims to all teachers at the school at a brief meeting, followed by a more specific meeting with the school's social services team which, like Heron High, consisted of senior managers, a school nurse and chaplain, the school psychologist, and an administration officer. One of the managers introduced his team to me as "the group that often has the job of mopping up the mess." The other manager appeared disgruntled at my presence at this meeting. Other team members, even though more supportive, were silenced by the efficiency of the managers in getting me out of the meeting. They proceeded to inform me that their team would generate a list of 45 students identified as "at risk" of failing school.

Having obtained formal ethics approval and access to the school and participants, I was not keen to take my research elsewhere. Staying the course required patience, perseverance, stamina, and support from significant others, including my supervisors, family, friends, and various researchers who understood the difficulties of conducting research in schools. This collegiality helped me to break through various gatekeepers, or what is sometimes referred to as the "rite of passage" (Rist, 1981, p. 266), to finally interview students:

> Talking it over with other researchers. Seeing the soft vulnerable spaces as opportunities rather than wounds. Trying to take part in the community rather than be a suspicious outsider. Instead, looking for gaps, spaces. Understanding the culture of resistance. Teasing out the deliberate from the imagined. Visioning. Some of those resistances are the only way to stay sane in an institution. Maybe these policies provide structure/instructions/simplistic answers as schools struggle to function. Instead, I will try to build relationships. Consider walls of strength, not as bricks but plastic strips. I will try to allow for people's subjectivities—I seem to be listening and reacting to the dominant voices, not necessarily the ones that will assist. There is some

urgency that I try to work through this and interview now, whilst this still feels to be an authentic and well-intended study. Maybe I should search for some supportive Year 10 teachers. (Research journal, May 2007)

The outcome of this process was that a leader of the Year 10 cohort responded to my persistent emails to inform me that I had a group of 30 students who had returned their consent forms and given permission for me to interview them. These students had been randomly selected by the school across the total of eight different classes in the year group as a part of their compulsory community services unit. I heard from some students later that a few of their friends had wanted to be interviewed; however, they did not have consent forms signed on the day that they were called up. Although this process was frustrating for me at the time, I was nevertheless pleased as an outside researcher to finally have been granted the opportunity to enter the school and do what I had long awaited: to hear the voices of the students themselves! In the following subsections I share some of this ethnographic journey via four dominant disciplinary strategies. These were: codes of conduct leading to exclusion; Good Standing and uniform policies leading to further conflicts; monitoring and surveillance and, finally, students being warehoused into other places.

Disciplinary Strategy One: Codes of Conduct and Exclusion

Public secondary schools like Anchorage were instructed by the Western Australian Government Education Department (WADET, 2001) to "consider key values of learning, equity, excellence and care" to develop and implement their own "Behaviour Management Plan" (p. 1). These core values often caused conflict as they were contradictory, especially around the notion of achieving academic excellence based on narrowly conceived standardized test scores. The Good Standing Policy at Anchorage, as part of the school's Behavior Management Plan, outlined what was expected of them as students and rewarded for exemplary behavior, attendance and work ethic. The policy also made it clear that when a student was 'out' of Good Standing that their privileges would be removed, and they would be monitored by their form [room] teachers. The values of equity and caring had been superseded by rewards for compliance and good order.

To define positive or negative behaviors (or choices), each government school's Good Standing Policy would be "accompanied by a description of the consequences and sanctions" (WADET, 2001, p. 6). This was to be known as a "code of conduct." This rigid collection of rules and regulations, when enacted at the school level, proved problematic for many of the young people I interviewed. For example, Anchorage's "code of conduct" listed responsibilities that included directives that students "come to school", "obey school rules" and "behave so as to uphold the reputation of the school".

Like many public schools struggling the rhetoric of engaged learning, equity, excellence and care, had morphed into a discourse and culture of compliance, order, and control as the focus on behavior, discipline, and performance escalated and the marketable image of the school intensified. Whitty (2002) explains that schools like Anchorage and Heron High are "ill-placed to capitalise on their market position" and therefore "the devolution of responsibility leads to the devolution of blame" (p. 13). As Chomsky (2003) argues, "this is pretty much what schools are like—they reward discipline and obedience, and they punish independence of the mind" (p. 28).

It was no surprise then, that by 2006, violations of the code of conduct became one of the two categories with the highest incidence of suspensions in Western Australian public schools (WADET, 2007b), and again the following year, 25% of total suspensions were also for violations of a school's code of conduct (WADET, 2009). This trend continued. In 2009, suspensions increased (with 12,529 suspensions over the year), yet the Director-General continued to claim that this was due to "the tougher stance taken on disruptive behaviour and that because more than half (57.2%) of those students had only been suspended once, they had learned their lesson" (WADET, 2010). In 2012 and 2013, "violations of the school Code of Conduct" (28.2%) remained one of the most common reasons for suspension (WADE, 2014, p. 32).

Disciplinary Strategy Two: "Good Standing" and Uniform Policies ("It's Not Hard to Get into Trouble")

Smyth et al. (2004), based on their extensive interviews with young people, explain that one of the ways schools "regulated student identities" is through the disciplining of school uniform (p. 76). Their research was echoed by many of the students I interviewed at Anchorage, for example:

BRAD: I was wearing pants that had faded a lighter color and the teacher made me go and get a uniform pass.

JENNY: Same with jumpers; you are not even allowed to wear them. Like if they are the wrong color and it is cold, you have to take it off.

GARY: It happened three weeks ago. I refused to take my jumper off. The teacher kept telling me to take it off because it wasn't uniform, and I had a cold at the time, so I didn't want to take it off.

NORA: Some of the rules are stupid so no-one follows them because they are so silly, so there is no point. Like that uniform rule, not eating in class, having to always ask to go to the toilet.

EVAN: I had these dark shorts. Everyone kept telling me that they were blue (school color) so I did not think I would get into trouble, but as soon as I went into class, I got sent out to get a dress pass.

As Connell (1985, p. 105) confirms, this emphasis on control is the side of school life that students resent the most. The emotional and social identity formation of young people is easily overlooked when sanctions are inflexible, punitive, irrelevant, and demeaning. Stu explained: "It's not hard to get into trouble. Like attendance, if you have three unexplained absences, you lose your 'Good Standing'. But sometimes the teachers just forget to mark the roll. You come late, so they don't mark you present" (Interview with Stu, August 2007).

Shane, another of the students from Anchorage, had also lost his "Good Standing" because he was considered "out" of school uniform. Anchorage's uniform was a simple white tee shirt with the school logo screen printed on it. Like Heron High, Anchorage was also focusing on their promotional "image" including a coat of arms printed on school bulletins, pamphlets, and entrance billboards. In Shane's situation, the focus on the image he presented, rather than on his situation, meant that his difficult life circumstances were not taken into consideration. Shane had just moved house during a family crisis and his grandparents were trying to help him. This was a cycle of crisis that Shane had been trying to break during his high school years, as he had already been excluded from school at the young age of eleven years when acting out because of the trauma of his mother being imprisoned. In the portrait of Shane below, compiled after two short interview sessions I had with him, a complex picture emerges of a young man trying to do the best that he can:

> I was expelled because I bashed a guy. I was in Year 6, and my Mum was going to court that day and probably going to jail and did end up going to jail. That day I was sitting in school really depressed then this guy said, "What is wrong with you? Get over it, just cause your Mum is going to jail." Then I just knocked him off his chair and beat the "crap out of him."
>
> My family is so confusing; it is like a trivia game or something. I have so many stepparents and parents, and now I have moved to live with my grandparents because I can no longer live with my parents, and it is a lot easier there. Now there is just me and my two younger brothers, even though sometimes they drive me mad.

It is easier now that I am living with my grandparents and I can get on with my schooling, but when I was living at my Mum's it wasn't easy because of the lifestyle there. It was bad. The teachers didn't understand that I was getting into trouble all the time because of things like not waking up on time or getting to bed late. My Mum is slack; she did not care if I went to school or not. Even though it is okay to have a day off school, it is not good two days out of every week. It gets boring. That is why I changed that, and I moved out, so I could do better. So far it is working.

It just makes you angry having to fill out this attendance blue sheet every day. It means you don't want to come to school so you just stay at home. I have had letters sent home only about my attendance. I have been getting into lots of trouble at home because the teachers have said that I haven't been there when I have. They mark me absent and then my family think that I have been "wagging" [absent from school].

Also, if you haven't explained with a note why you are out of uniform then you get detention. I tried to explain to Mr. B from Student Services when he came up to me [...] "Look, I don't know where my shirt is, I think my sister might have stolen it off me because I don't live with her anymore, so my school top is obviously lost somewhere around there." I was going to buy a new one, but I have already spent the money today on lunch. I did try to explain to Mr. B but he said I would have to do detention anyway. I am trying really hard to get my "Good Standing" back so that I can go to the end-of-year function. (Interviews with Shane, July and August 2007)

This is a portrait of a sophisticated young man, experiencing multiple contextual and complex problems on top of dealing with punitive rules and regulations when attending compulsory schooling. Ladson-Billings (2014) explains that "schools, which should provide opportunities for widening the world," are instead "places where their worlds bec[ome] increasingly constrained and narrow" (p. 10).

Jen, a good friend of Shane, also found herself "in trouble" as the enactment of behavior and discipline policies became increasingly incongruent with her personal needs. Jen also had a difficult home situation very early on in her life. Like Shane, she had often clashed with the majority of her teachers and became disengaged as she became singled out for not complying with issues of appearance, conformity, and regimented time schedules. The "institutional approach to discipline" (Slee, 1991) in schools has little time or inclination to understand the circumstances and needs of a 15-year-old girl who had been kidnapped at two years of age by her estranged father and shunted back and forth between three different states of Australia. Often, it was difficult for her to attend school because of her unstable home life, and when she did attend school, it was mainly to meet up with friends and have some reassurance from them that she was coping with her own life circumstances: "I lost my 'Good Standing' for being out of uniform. Last year I only came for a few weeks because I just could not be bothered trying to get it back" (Interview with Jen, August 2007).

Generally, Jen did not attend formal lessons during my time visiting Anchorage and spent most of her days at home fending for herself. As an ethnographic researcher, I felt privileged to spend time with her and share some of her life story to better understand the challenging and complex circumstances many young people find themselves in through no fault of their own. As schools hunker down to further tighten control around students' use of space and time, then as many of the students explain, "it's not hard to get into trouble" because being punctual, lining up in order, wearing the correct uniform, focus on personal appearance and choice of hairstyle, the painting of nails and wearing of jewelry, all became power struggles which often result in conflict between students and some of their teachers. Stevenson and Ellsworth (1993) elaborate:

> High schools, as organizations responsible for the welfare of a large and diverse number of adolescents, are confronted with a difficult task in establishing and enforcing rules for orderly and acceptable behaviour. When these rules have the potential for exacerbating the problem, or creating additional problems for the student to which they are being applied, then the rules themselves, or their uniform and rigid application, need to be re-examined. (p. 266)

Disciplinary Strategy Three: Monitoring and Surveillance

When a student is out of "Good Standing" their status is consequently recorded on the school's SIS data. The Western Australian Education Department had contracted RM Asia-Pacific Pty Ltd to provide this web-based software management system as a mechanism for government schools to easily and smoothy record, monitor, and report on student behavior and attendance. It was piloted in several schools in 1999–2000, and by the following year, SIS was rolled out to all schools, including Anchorage.

Data for "Good Standing" at both Anchorage and Heron High is initially monitored by classroom teachers who enter records of student behavior (usually relating to dress code, lateness, and truancy) onto the system whenever they have the opportunity. Students lose their "Good Standing" after three unexplained absences, or three negative behavior records; for example, "out of uniform". They are subsequently "case managed" by the Student Services Department of the school. Once there is a loss of "Good Standing," the student is issued a behavior report card for a week, and then additional weeks until it is completed correctly. An example of a typical style of card is illustrated below:

Behaviour						
Good Standing Report Card						
Name _____						
Form No _____ Date _____						
Day	1	2	3	4	5	Parent Signature
Monday						
Tuesday						
Wednesday						
Thursday						
Friday						
Teacher to tick and sign if student behaviour appropriate and cross if inappropriate						

Each classroom teacher, in each period of each day (i.e., 25 times per week) has to endorse and sign this card, regulating and scrutinizing each student's attendance and actions. The parent (if there is a parent) is also subject to surveillance by having to "sign off" at the end of everyday. This scrupulous reporting and labeling process is not only humiliating for many students and their families but was also a distracting administrative task for teachers.

My reflective journal notes below elaborate on how behavior and discipline policies often manifest within schools, marginalizing and disempowering students; initially via the "Good Standing" and uniform policies, and then the permanent and powerful surveillance of databases collecting their personal information:

> The theme of "being monitored," especially around use of mobiles, attendance, and uniform on SIS allowed me to frame the student stories of how they had been under surveillance, what they could and could not say and do, what they could look like, speak, and how they could use their bodies. The control of their use of space (on an oval only if in uniform), their conduct in canteen formations, the lining up outside class, their use of time; timetable of five- or six-hour slots, odd timings; their breaks, even their home lives were being monitored! This use of SIS to record the students who had threatened or disturbed the peace, the quiet, the compliant unit of the classroom or conduct on the sports field, the canteen—these were the ones that had their names recorded on the data screen to be stored and viewed forever.
>
> Every time they were out of "Good Standing" or in detention it was recorded. And really, what did this crime mean? Stealing? Bashing? Cheating? No, none of those; it was for not wearing the correct color shirt, being one minute late to another boring math lesson or talking to one of their friends instead of listening to a teacher

they didn't respect. Now I feel confident in saying that what helped determine how I used their stories into themes was to consider "freedom"—the expansion of students' voices because they were telling me loud and clear that they were fed up with being watched, contained, and controlled. (Research journal, August 2008)

Disciplinary Strategy Four: Warehousing of Students

In Chapter 3, I discussed the outsourcing of behavior hubs for those students who had been excluded from public secondary schools. These hubs, known as Curriculum and Re-engagement in Education (CARE) schools, are managed by private companies or charities and receive government funding. One of the first of these schools was established in the Anchorage region in 2008. These CARE schools, which focused on vocational programs and smaller classes, increased to six new campuses in the region in 2016, and then by 2019 consisted of 450 students (Hiatt & Mitchell, 2021, p. 20).

The headlines of *The West Australian* newspaper at the beginning of the school year in 2021 highlighted that "troubled kids are big business" with the growth of new forms of privatized/government subsidized alternative schooling in the area (Hiatt & Mitchell, 2021, p. 20). The real reason that the Anchorage CARE school hit the media, however, was a sensationalized incident at the school, drawing attention to "violence and trouble," a recurring theme in the media at this time.

The next section draws together the dominant themes that emerged from the ethnographic data shared throughout this chapter. In summary, I argue that behavior and discipline policies and practices often lead to a culture of compliance, performance, and marketability rather than the espoused values of "learning, equity, excellence and care," as stated in official policy documents. As a result, it is hardly surprising to see students both overtly and covertly resisting punitive rules and regulations by "dropping out, drifting off, [and] being excluded" from schooling (Smyth et al., 2004). In contrast, the student narratives shared throughout this chapter reveal that what matters most to students is the relationships and sense of belonging they have with teachers, school, and the wider community.

Key Themes from Anchorage High

Young people are largely missing from formal policy and political debates regarding matters of public interest and issues of direct interest to them. (Bessant et al., 2017, p. 176)

Theme One: Compliance, Resistance, and Dropping Out

Anchorage's Behavior Management Plan (BMP), following the directives from the Education Department's Behavior Management in Schools Policy (WADET, 2001), determined that students must "come to school," "obey school rules," and "behave so as to uphold the reputation of the school"). The key values stated in the policy of learning, equity, excellence, and care were swiftly interpreted and enacted at the school level into a list of rigid rules with an emphasis on compliance, performance, and upholding the school's reputation and marketable image. In other words, students were not only forced to attend school, but also to be proud of a school that was often at odds with their own needs and interests. As Dewey (1916/1966) put it over 100 years ago:

> The chief source of the "problem of discipline" in schools is that the teacher has often to spend the large part of the time in suppressing the bodily activities which take the mind away from its material. A premium is put on physical quietude; on silence, on rigid uniformity of posture and movement; upon a machine-like simulation of the attitudes of intelligent interest. The teachers' business is to hold the pupils up to these requirements and to punish the inevitable deviations which occur. (p. 141)

In the context of zero tolerance or "get tough" approaches to school discipline, teachers and school administrators were forced to manage and isolate those students who were not obedient, not performing, or not promoting the best image of the school. For these students, there appeared to be no other option; hence escalating levels of resistance leading to exclusion. Shor (1992) explains that student behavior is often "provoked, driven underground, where it becomes a subterranean source of acting out" (p. 24). Gary explained:

> If only they did not make such a big deal, I would probably be able to do what they want, but they wear me down, make such a big deal that it is easier if I just *don't* do what they want. At least then I can be a winner somehow!
> If they were not so strict on it, most people would probably wear school uniform. It is just rebellion. Most people want to be rebellious. It's like you want us to do one thing, but we are going to do the opposite. If they weren't so strict on it, I would probably buy the uniform. But I choose not to, to annoy them! I like "pissing the teachers off" about it. (Interviews with Gary, June and July 2007)

School uniform had become "a site of contestation" (Smyth et al., 2004, p. 177) for Gary, as it impacted on his sense of identity, and therefore he was "prepared to endure detentions for infractions" (p. 76). As behavior management and school discipline policies morph into rigidly enforced codes of conduct it is easy to see how students like Gary became collateral damage and quickly lose their "Good Standing." The Department of Education's new "dress requirements for students in WA public schools" (WADET, 2007a) was endorsed during this time, with the Minister of Education claiming that "traditional styles of uniform will play an important part in keeping up the strong reputation of public schools and ensuring parents continue to send their children to public schools" (2007a, p. 1). Even more restrictive in this policy was the statement that, "if a matter cannot be resolved with non-compliance of the dress code at the school, the principal may apply sanctions prescribed in the School Education Regulations 2000" (WADET, 2007a, p. 7).

This policy meant that Gary was unable to participate in school excursions, or reward days, and could only "be a winner somehow" by not conforming. Gary was looking forward to the end-of-term function, marking the end of a decade of schooling together with his friends. However, by the time I interviewed Gary for a second time, he had been in so much trouble that he had been placed on an "Individual Education Plan" for behavior management. By the third visit, two months later, and only halfway through the school year, Gary had left. While official claims that dress codes promote a "positive image" and a "sense of identity" (WADET, 2007a, p. 1), for many students like Gary, "looking the part [...] often *keeps* students from attending school" (Ladson-Billings, 2014, p. 8).

Students like Gary do not leave school because they have gone through the entire official Good Standing Policy process, which after the report card stage, involves panel meetings with parents, case conferences, support staff, district office representatives, and other agencies. No, Gary had left because he had already experienced enough at the report card stage, because mechanisms and methods of behavioristic discipline approaches had spread "throughout the whole social body" (Foucault, 1979, p. 209).

As we really listen to what these young people are saying, a pattern emerges. Firstly, disenchantment occurs, followed by a snowball effect of failing and falling deeper into a vortex of powerlessness, further marginalization, unhealthy relationships, and destructive interactions within the school. When the control of students becomes the priority then it is not difficult for students who do not comply with the code of conduct to be labeled as "difficult" or "pointy end," resulting in a downward spiral of conflict with their teachers, increasing truancy (Riley et al., 2002), and insensitivity to students' emerging adult status (Stevenson & Ellsworth, 1993, p. 260). Gary was one of these students.

Theme Two: Relationships and "Belonging"

> Young people are going to school to be with their friends. (Smyth et al., 2004, p. 87)

> The same expansion of horizons which marks youth as a time of emergent and enhanced individuality also provides a broader context for affiliation and belonging. (Hall et al., 1999, p. 509)

Smyth et al. (2004) found that for the many young people they interviewed, there was a tension between "getting on with schoolwork" (the identity of the successful) and "sustaining/nurturing an identity through intimate relationships" (p. 87). Kia explained:

> If I was in S&E right now, that teacher and me just don't get along; if I was in there now [instead of talking with you], I probably would have lost it. Today I am not in the best of moods, cause last night my Mum kicked me out and I am living with my Dad at the moment. So today if the teacher just niggled, I would "lose it"!

During this same interview, Kia also expressed how important a healthy relationship could have been: "We learn from teachers who know how you are feeling and will have a little joke with you."

Meier (2002) explains the importance of personal trust and seeking commonalities in relationships between teachers and students; a "hard-won, democratic trust" (p. 3) as expressed by other students I interviewed:

NIC: The teachers I respect, like my English teacher, he helped me through everything. Like my English isn't really all that good and he helped me, then it really improved.

EV: My Year 8 English teacher, she was a great help. She found out that I was one of the best spellers that she has ever known. I was a better speller than her Year 11 students; that made me feel good.

KYLIE: Ms. B saw that, and she helped develop me into a better person. She actually cared, and she was there if any of us needed someone to talk to. She is just so human, and she cradles you through high school.

DANIEL: Some teachers let you talk and listen to music, yet we still do our work. We respect them by doing our work because they respect us.

When students have an opportunity to express what is going on inside their own lives, there is a greater chance that they will respect their teachers and their schooling. Smyth (2006, p. 45) terms this the "social glue" holding things together. In a similar way, Connell (2015) explains the significance of relationships as a key ingredient in the complex process of learning: "The capacity for care is deeply involved, that is indeed the basis of the creativity of teaching. An educational encounter implies a relationship of respect between teacher and learner, which requires a kind of mutual citizenship in the situation" (p. 187).

Insights from the Ethnographic Field: In Conclusion

In listening to the student narratives from Anchorage and my own ethnographic insights from Heron High in the previous chapter, important understandings can be shared that speak directly from the field (Coffey, 2018). As Cook-Sather (2002) argues, by genuinely authorizing young people's perspectives, we also provide the "legitimate and valued spaces" for them to speak, "re-tuning our ears so that we can hear what they say, and redirecting our actions in response to what we hear" (p. 4). Below, I summarize three important insights I have gleaned from Chapters 4 and 5:

- Zero tolerance or "get tough" approaches to behavior management and discipline policy are largely ineffective and have a disproportionate impact on the most vulnerable students.
- Negative media sensationalism and misrepresentation of young people and the kinds of policies enacted in schools create further and longer lasting problems for these young people.
- Marginalized students, often living in complex situations, have some urgent messages for policy makers at all levels about what works best for them.

Insight One: Zero Tolerance (Getting Tough) Does Not Work, Especially for Those Who Are Most Vulnerable

Many students I interviewed believe that "getting tough," "drawing lines in the sand," and "grit pedagogy" (Saltman, 2014) do not work. Quick fixes and 10-point action plans (WADE, 2018, 2023) only exacerbate the situation for them. These behavioristic systems violate the rights of many young people, their freedom, and their identity formation, resulting in more conflict, greater resistance, and students responding by either "opting out" or resisting, culminating in escalating conflicts and ultimately suspensions and exclusions. Freire (2005) explains this response to oppression as the "rebellion they express, as they emerge in the historical process," which is "motivated by that desire to act effectively" (Freire, 2005, p. 78).

Obtaining respect is complex, as the "changing nature of students" (Smyth et al., 2004, p. 77) and a well-developed sense of justice mean that many students expect more nuanced and democratic ways of relating with school authorities, rather than simply doing as they are told. As Down et al. (2024) explain, "common-sense policy discourses" such as behavior management and student exclusion "construct the problem of disaffected students" (p. 2). The United States' experience with "zero tolerance" policies demonstrates that, once these young people are pushed out of classrooms, other complications follow, funneling them into a "pipeline" of juvenile and criminal justice systems. The non-profit advocacy organization the Advancement Project summarizes these extensive problems:

> Denial of education through increased suspension and expulsion rates, referrals to inadequate alternative schools, lower test scores, higher dropout rates, and racial profiling of students. [...] Once many of these youths are in "the system," they never get back on the academic track. Sometimes, schools refuse to readmit them; and even if these students do return to school, they are often labeled and targeted for close monitoring by school staff and police. Consequently, many become demoralized, drop out, and fall deeper and deeper into the juvenile or criminal justice systems. Those who do not drop out may find that their discipline and juvenile or criminal records haunt them when they apply to college or for a scholarship or government grant or try to enlist in the military or find employment. In some places, a criminal record may prevent them or their families from residing in publicly subsidized housing. In this era of zero tolerance, the consequences of child or adolescent behaviors may long outlive students' teenage years. (2005, p. 12, as cited in Heitzeg, 2018, p. 28)

Insight Two: Media Misrepresentation Creates More Problems

At both Anchorage and Heron High, the local media sensationalized incidents at the schools, with headlines of "youth crime" and "behaviour lacking," without investigating the complexity of what was going on in the lives of the young people themselves and without understanding what led to the incidents. Research by Berndtsson (2019) in Sweden highlights that this type of "sensationalism" marginalizes disadvantaged students in particular: "These media depictions are mostly taken from segregated suburban, low-income areas. Schools in ethnic white middle-class areas rarely end up in these 'journalistic dramas', regardless of the fact that school violence is not merely a suburban phenomenon" (p. 97).

The current media and consequential political discourses around issues of declining standards, discipline, and control play a part in constructing the "deviant" and out-of-control youth. According to Kelly (2001, pp. 24–25), such discourses are a historical leftover. It is therefore timely to listen to what students themselves have to say, instead of being swayed by the popular and dominant media responses.

Insight Three: What Works for Students: Young People Have Urgent and Important Messages

Listening to the voices of the students and what they tell us about the significance of dialogic relations, it becomes clear that school discipline and behavior management policies need to be reframed and reconstructed to foster relationship (trust, care and respect *in* and *with* them) (Freire, 2005, p. 75). Schultz (2008) describes how he was able to achieve respect with his students:

> With a commitment to building relationships in my classroom and with the community, I pursued ways to learn about their daily lives as an outsider. I saw myself in many ways as a student of my students; able to learn from them by sharing. (p. 145)

As Smyth (2006) explains, reciprocal respect and trust are "crucial bridging mechanisms" (p. 45) in developing a healthy active school culture through which complex learning occurs (Connell, 2015, p. 187). The young people throughout this chapter have shared what works for them and what does not in their experiences, understandings, and interpretations of behavior and discipline policies in their lives at school. Smyth and Hattam (2002) and Smyth et al. (2004) collected and shared the voices of numerous young people who left secondary school way too early because they had been shoved out. Their findings reflect the messages that emerged from the voices of the young people interviewed at Anchorage and the observations recorded from Heron High, and that is that many young people would have been more likely to stay engaged within their respective schools, and become "somebody," if they had experienced a culture that allowed them to:

- be treated with respect and be encouraged to develop workable relationships with teachers and other students;
- have a say in matters like school uniform;

- be listened to and have their wishes and interests taken into account in choice of subjects and scheduling of assignments;
- be treated fairly and consistently in discipline policies;
- have issues of harassment by teachers and students taken seriously; and
- be empathetically listened to and heard regarding the complexity and individuality of their lives (Smyth & Hattam, 2002, p. 385).

In the next chapter, I discuss ways to provide hope in accommodating these young people in a culture of learning in schools that permits them to "become somebody" (Wexler, 1992).

References

Beach, D., & Vigo-Arrazola, B. (2021). Critical ethnographies of education and for social and educational transformation: A meta-ethnography. *Qualitative Inquiry*, 27(6), 677–688.

Berndtsson, K. H. (2019). Segregation, class, "race" and school violence. In J. Lunneblad (Ed.), *Policing schools: School violence and the juridification of youth, young people and learning processes in school and everyday life* (pp. 97–111). Springer Nature.

Bessant, J., Farthing, R., & Watts, R. (2017). *The precarious generation: A political economy of young people*. Routledge.

Burgess, R. (1988). Conversations with a purpose: The ethnographic interview in educational research. *Studies in Qualitative Methodology*, 1(1), 137–155.

Chomsky, N. (2003). The function of schools: Subtler and cruder methods of control. In K. J. Saltman & D. Gabbard (Eds.), *Education as enforcement: The militarization and corporatization of schools* (pp. 25–35). RoutledgeFalmer.

Coffey, A. (2018). *Doing ethnography*. Sage.

Connell, R. W. (1985). *Teachers' work*. George Allen & Unwin.

Connell, R. (2015). Markets all around: Defending education in a neoliberal time. In H. Proctor, P. Brownlee, & P. Freebody (Eds.), *Controversies in education: Orthodoxy and heresy in policy and practice* (pp. 181–197). Springer International Publishing.

Cook-Sather, A. (2002). Authorizing students' perspectives: Toward trust, dialogue, and change in education. *Educational Researcher*, 31(4), 3–14.

Dewey, J. (1966). *Democracy and education: An introduction to the philosophy of education*. Free Press. (Original work published 1916).

Down, B., Sullivan, A., Tippett, N., Johnson, B., Manolev, J., & Robinson, J. (2024). What is missing in policy discourses about school exclusions? *Critical Studies in Education*. Advance online publication. https://doi.org/10.1080/17508487.2024.2312878

Foucault, M. (1979). *Discipline and punish: The birth of the prison* (A. Sheridan, Trans.). Peregrine. (Original work published 1975).

Freire, P. (2005). *Pedagogy of the oppressed* (M. B. Ramos, Trans.). Continuum. (Original work published 1970).

Hall, T., Coffey, A., & Williamson, H. (1999). Self, space and place: Youth identities and citizenship. *British Journal of Sociology of Education, 20*(4), 501–513.

Heitzeg, N. A. (2018). Criminalizing education: Zero tolerance policies, police in the hallways, and the school to prison pipeline. In A. J. Nocella II, P. Parmar, & D. Stovall (Eds.), *From education to incarceration: Dismantling the school-to-prison pipeline* (2nd ed., pp. 17–41). Peter Lang.

Hiatt, B., & Mitchell, R. (2021, February 27). Troubled kids are big business: Rapid growth in new type of private school. *The West Australian*, 20–21.

Kelly, P. (2001). Youth at risk: Processes of individualisation and responsibilisation in the risk society. *Discourse: Studies in the Cultural Politics of Education, 22*(1), 23–33.

Ladson-Billings, G. (2014). The pedagogy of poverty: The big lies about poor children. In P. C. Gorski & K. Zenkov (Eds.), *The big lies of school reform: Finding better solutions for the future of public education* (pp. 7–16). Routledge.

Madison, D. S. (2005). *Critical ethnography: Method, ethics, and performance*. Sage.

Meier, D. (2002). *In schools we trust: Creating communities of learning in an era of testing and standardization*. Beacon Press.

Riley, K., Rustique-Forrester, E., Fuller, M., Rowles, D., Leth, R., & Docking, J. (2002). *Working with disaffected students: Why students lose interest in school and what we can do about it*. Paul Chapman.

Rist, R. (1981). On what we know (or think we do): Gatekeeping and the social control of knowledge. In T. Popkewitz & B. Tabachnick (Eds.), *The study of schooling: Field based methodologies in educational research and evaluation* (pp. 264–275). Praeger.

Robinson, J. (2011). *"Troubling" behaviour management: listening to student voice* [Ph.D. thesis]. Murdoch University.

Russell, L. (2013). Researching marginalised young people. *Ethnography and Education, 8*(1), 46–60.

Saltman, K. J. (2014). The austerity school: Grit, character, and the privatization of public education. *Symploke, 22*(1–2), 41–57.

Schultz, B. (2008). *Spectacular things happen along the way: Lessons from an urban classroom*. Teachers College Press.

Shor, I. (1992). *Empowering education: Critical teaching for social change*. University of Chicago Press.

Slee, R. (1991). Institutional approaches to discipline. In M. Lovegrove & R. Lewis (Eds.), *Classroom discipline* (pp. 145–172). Longman Cheshire.

Smyth, J. (2006). Researching teachers working with young adolescents: Implications for ethnographic research. *Ethnography and Education, 1*(1), 31–51.

Smyth, J., & Hattam. R. (2002). Early school leaving and the cultural geography of high schools. *British Educational Research Journal, 28*(3), 375–397.

Smyth, J., & Hattam, R., with Cannon, J., Edwards, J., Wilson, N., & Wurst, S. (2004). *Dropping out, drifting off, being excluded: Becoming somebody without school*. Peter Lang.

Stevenson, R., & Ellsworth, J. (1993). Dropouts and the silencing of critical voices. In L. Weis & M. Fine (Eds.), *Beyond silenced voices: Class, race, and gender in United States schools* (pp. 259–271). State University of New York Press.

Tanton, R., Dare, L., Miranti, R., Vidyattama, Y., Yule, A., & McCabe, M. (2021). *Dropping Off the Edge 2021: Persistent and multilayered disadvantage in Australia*. Melbourne: Jesuit Social Services.

Welch, A. (2022). Making education policy. In A. Welch et al. (Eds.), *Education, change and society* (5th ed., pp. 247–281). Oxford University Press.

Western Australian Department of Education (WADE). (2014). *Annual report 2012–13*.

Western Australian Department of Education (WADE). (2018). *Let's take a stand together: Minister's statement on school violence*.

Western Australian Department of Education (WADE). (2023). *Shaping the future: Standing together against violence: Minister's statement on how families can help keep schools safe*.

Western Australian Department of Education and Training (WADET). (2001). *Behaviour management in schools*.

Western Australian Department of Education and Training (WADET). (2007a). *Dress requirements for students in WA public schools*.

Western Australian Department of Education and Training (WADET). (2007b, August 27). School suspensions and exclusions under the spotlight [Media release].

Western Australian Department of Education and Training (WADET). (2009, November 4). School suspensions continue to improve student behaviour [Media release].

Western Australian Department of Education and Training (WADET). (2010, May 21). Suspensions increase as tough stance on bad behaviour continues [Media release].

Wexler, P. (1992). *Becoming somebody: Toward a social psychology of school*. Falmer Press.

Whitty, G. (2002). *Making sense of education policy: Studies in the sociology and politics of education*. Paul Chapman.

Youdell, D. (2006). *Impossible bodies, impossible selves: Exclusions and student subjectivities*. Springer Netherlands.

· 6 ·

HOPE FOR TRANSFORMATION: FINDING THE RELATIONAL

Introduction: Opportunities for the Relational

The previous chapters have "troubled" and critiqued the discipline policies and practices evolving during neoliberal times. Policies do not always provide schools with clear guidance, especially when "the range of options available in deciding what to do are narrowed or changed, or particular goals or outcomes are set" (Ball, 1994, p. 19).

The purpose of this chapter is to maintain hope and seek out the relational because as Freire (1997) explains "without a vision for tomorrow, hope is impossible" (p. 13). Hickey and Riddle (2023) and Cook-Sather (2002) also express that this is challenging, and difficult work as systemic and structural educational changes and dynamics have reduced the importance of relationships in schools and have prioritized "achievement and behaviour outcomes" (Hickey & Riddle, 2023, p. 9). These difficulties, however, can also be viewed as opportunities to search for and create more inclusive and democratic pedagogies and practices, "opening opportunities for teachers and students, and students as peers, to come together" in relational encounters (Hickey & Riddle, 2023, p. 11).

The rethinking and "releasing" of the social imagination (Greene, 1995) of a relationally engaging school is authentic, because it has "the capacity to invent visions of what should be and what might be" (Greene, 1995, p. 5). This thinking is contextual, and therefore not an arbitrary "means to an end" (Riddle & Hickey, 2023, pp. 275, 277).

The struggle for democratic change requires attention to the nuances and particularities of how relationships are formed (Riddle & Hickey, 2023, p. 279). Throughout this chapter, the particularities and nuances of the personal voices of the young people interviewed provide transformative hope. Fromm (1968) encourages this, because "to hope means to be ready at every moment for that which is not yet born, and yet not become desperate if there is no birth in our lifetime" (p. 9).

The Art of Loving

Fromm (1956) argued that the principle of loving is incompatible with capitalist society as "an increasing number of people cease to be *independent* and become *dependent* on the managers of the great economic empires" (p. 131, emphasis added), alienated from ourselves, our fellow human beings, and from nature (pp. 132, 158). Fromm (1981/2010) continued to argue throughout his book *On Disobedience* that as critical social researchers we can learn to be radical, and to evolve as humans requires certain acts of disobedience:

> It is not primarily an attitude directed *against* something, but *for* something: for man's [sic] capacity to see, to say what he sees, and to refuse to say what he does not see. To do so he does not need to be aggressive or rebellious; he needs to have his eyes open, to be fully awake, and willing to take the responsibility to open the eyes of those who are in danger of perishing because they are half asleep. (Fromm 1981/2010, n.p.)

Erich Fromm is one of the most cited critical theorists in Paulo Freire's (1970/2005) book *Pedagogy of the oppressed* and indeed their paths crossed over the years (Darder, 2018, p. 76). Freire's notion of education as the practice of freedom continues Fromm's pathway to critical hope because it denies that humans are "abstract, isolated, independent and unattached to the world; it denies that the world exists as a reality apart from people" (Freire, 1970/2005, p. 81).

Keeping Hope Alive

It is the task of the living to keep hope alive. (Bauman, 2006, p. 160)

> Daydreaming, reflecting, letting the sun play with the leaves . . .
> Patterns flickering in an out of my head . . .
> Spaces to imagine . . .
> Time to collect precious moments.
> As ideas fall into the vacuum,
> Letting go and waiting for stillness.
> Moments captured held and cherished.
> What is it?
> Hope?
>
> When the pen hits the paper,
> First it moves randomly.
> Then it finds its place and connection
> To the surface and the ink
> Creating its own picture;
> One of meaning and ideas framed.
>
> When the pen hits the paper
> And the ink flows
> Then the writing is both passion and fury
> Sometimes gently
> Other times turbulent, blocked and sliding in and out of focus.
> What is this?
> It is hope for transformation. (Journal entry, November 2010)

Simon (1992) explains that hope is more than my poetic, wishful daydreaming expressed here as I search an "openness above all to possibilities for human attachments, expressions, and assertions" (p. 3). In being hopeful, Simon (1992, p. 3) suggests I should not merely envisage and wish, but *act* "in the present," challenging neoliberal policies, practices, and procedures that marginalize. Simon (1992) explains: "hope is different from the wish in that it is a predisposition to action rather than merely a foretaste of pleasure. It grows from commitment to responsibility and not from a passive yearning for ultimate peace and resolution" (p. 4).

My commitment to responsibility is the ultimate aim of this book. I am writing it because it is my obligation, as an "enclave of resistance" (Smyth et al., 2009, p. 43), to provide hope and possibility of transformation by placing the young people, the schools they attend, and the communities in which they live at the forefront, not only the periphery. In this manner, teachers and their communities can begin to question those policy practices that are harmful and instead develop curricula which is engaging and inclusive, and builds capacity (Smyth et al., 2009, p. 19).

Releasing Our Imaginations

> Hope, as it happens, is so important for our existence, individual and social, that we must take every care not to experience it in a mistaken form, and thereby allow it to slip toward hopelessness. (Freire, 1992, p. 3)

Greene (2009) encourages us as educationalists to use our imagination, to "bring the light back into the dark times" because it "allows us to think of things as they could be otherwise" and envisage an alternative (p. 138). This imagination "opens spaces in experience where projects can be devised"—where they "ought to be" (p. 141). This vision also "imparts a conscious quality to experience and the realization that things do not repeat themselves" (p. 141). Greene (2009) explains this vision "enrich[es] and stimulate[s] through live encounters with others, through exposure to diverse vantage points and unfamiliar ways of looking at the world" (p. 142). As Kelly et al. (2019) confirm, "we need to become more inventive, more imaginative. We need to think. To re-think. And to do so again" (p. 212).

Paulo Freire (1997), similarly, used the following powerful, inspirational words on returning to Brazil after 15 years in exile: "Was I returning old? No. I was returning hopeful, motivated to relearn Brazil, to participate in the struggle for democracy and for public school to become popular school gradually, thus becoming less elitist, more critical, more open" (p. 33).

Horizons of Possibility

Simon (1992), inspired by the understandings of hope derived from Ernst Bloch, explains that not all "daydreaming" is insignificant because, as he quotes, "Bloch views daydreams as a radical questioning and a fleeting resonance of freedom, articulating the embodiment of alternative identities and a horizon of possibility" (p. 7). What then are these alternatives and horizons of possibility? In the following section, I investigate this notion of possibility by (i) using our imaginations to climb "out of the wreckage" (Monbiot, 2017), (ii) disrupting neoliberal policy and putting "the public" back in (Reid, 2019);

(iii) seeking new pedagogical directions, and (iv) reclaiming the relational in education (Riddle & Hickey, 2023).

Climbing Out of the Wreckage of Neoliberal Policy

> By confronting the politics of alienation with a politics of belonging, we rekindle our imagination and discover our power to act. (Monbiot, 2017, p. 183)

As Monbiot (2017) explains, "the only thing that can displace a story is a story" (p. 3). The neoliberal policy story or narrative that has been told regarding behavior and discipline in schools has been predominantly driven by "an economic system [. . .] a political system that promotes economic growth about all other aims, regardless of whether it enhances human welfare or damages it" (p. 19). The fallout of this system is the loss of our common purpose (Monbiot, 2017, p. 21) or common good (Reid, 2019, p. 178).

To climb out of this wreckage, the new story needs to be one of belonging and needs to consist of different values than those that presently dominate school behavior and discipline policies. When young people feel part of a community that welcomes them with compassion, empathy, equity, and respect then they are more likely to engage with society and with a world that offers hope and transformation. The field notes below, taken after my interview with Beth, a student from Anchorage High, keep hope alive:

> My final interview for the research was with Beth. The other students did not make it that day as there was some event on. Beth had been reserved and easily dominated by others when I first met her, and she was also "closed off" the first half of this interview. When I suggested she show me around the school I began to experience a more confident Beth within her own place in the school culture. It is as if she could find that gap, or interstices, as Stengers (2002, p. 257) coins it, a way to break the cycle of withdrawal of feeling and being touched by something. As other students recognized Beth they greeted and smiled at her as she gracefully ushered me through the library, the gym, the canteen, and any other social meeting pocket of the school. Throughout and within these spaces she had a real sense of pride of her place, even though, within the classrooms, things were not conducive to her learning, because there, the thinking and the feeling had been separated. (Field notes, August 2007)

What becomes evident in these notes is that for students like Beth to feel successful at school, there is a need to "belong" to the school and feel actively involved in meaningful and responsible ways. Affect and emotion play a most significant role in students' identity but also in creating a spirit of social collectiveness (Giroux, 2003, p. 164). This glimmer of social collectiveness that

I witnessed in a place and space for Beth created opportunities for alternative dialog (Lawrence-Lightfoot & Hoffmann Davis, 1997, p. 11) and "maps of meaning" (Giroux, 2003, p. 164). For example, when I asked Beth in this same interview what helped her to learn, she replied: "Sometimes when I am on my own and get on with my work, but other times when I am with my friends, and I can ask them something." Beth's experience provides hope of climbing "out of the wreckage" and creating a new story.

Putting "the Public" Back In

Greene (1982) confirms the importance of being together in public spaces, as Beth expressed in the previous section, allowing for plural, diverse, and distinctive ways of seeing and hearing the "sounds and tones of voices seldom listened to" (p. 9). The "true value of a public education can be measured only to the extent that it makes public life better for *all* citizens" (Duncan-Andrade & Morrell, 2008, p. 18, emphasis added).

Both Monbiot (2017) and Reid (2019) agree that we need a new story; a new narrative to underscore the importance of public education which has suffered enormously over the past four decades in Australia under neoliberalism. That is because so many government schools have been "moved from being seen as a public good for all, to being understood as a safety net for those who cannot afford private education" (Reid, 2019, p. 68). Unless the core neoliberal elements, the logic and the policy directions of school behavior and discipline policies are removed, new versions of the policies "will simply be subsumed by the same ideological baggage" (Reid, 2019, p. 288).

In the previous two chapters of this book, when tracing discipline policy practices and procedures within two large public secondary schools, I discussed many examples of neoliberal change imposed at both case study sites. These included new "models" of discipline such as Positive Behavior Support (PBS) and Multi-Tiered Implementation Systems (MTIS), in which students and their families are considered "clientele" and "customers" and those students who do not comply and maintain the good reputation of the school labeled "disruptive," issued "Individual Behavior Plans," and eventually leave or are removed from school. When the corporate model overrides the public good for all, a fundamental human right that could enable young people to flourish (Reid, 2019, p. 283), then it is time to ask some serious questions.

A place to begin challenging the corporate, economic, and political interference in schools is to revisit the Senate Education and Employment

References Committee (2023, 2024) report *The issue of increasing disruption in Australian school classrooms*. The Senate committee recommended in the interim report (2023) that the focus on behavior be strengthened by introducing a "Behaviour Curriculum" within the Australian Curriculum (Rec. 5.21, p. ix) and an annual national auditing system to measure its effectiveness like the "United Kingdom's National Behaviour Survey" (Rec. 5.39, p. 58). These are examples of what Reid (2019, p. 131) and Smyth (2001, p. 126) both term "policy borrowing."

The final report, *The issue of increasing disruption in classrooms* (Senate, Education and Employment References Committee, 2024), had one recommendation (Rec. 1.28, p. 9) which related to declining academic standards in Australian schools. These plans for future behavior curriculum and auditing systems to meet competing global academic standards not only need to be challenged; they need to be dismantled. It is time for new narratives and pedagogical directions!

New Pedagogical Directions

Replacing the private, competitive, and narrowing curriculum that focuses on performance targets, with a new vision of the public school, requires alternative narratives and pedagogical directions that engage students and are "non-exclusionary" (Simon, 1992, p. 94). This requires a new imaginary (Rizvi & Lingard, 2010), one that recognizes "human beings as social and cultural beings as well as economic ones" (p. 201).

This new imaginary, in place of "teaching" behavior, allows educators to "possess and model" their capacity "to think critically, flexibly and creatively" (Reid, 2019, p. 274) leading pedagogical directions that permeates the school and the systems driving it to be collaborative in decision making. Max van Manen (2002), in his small book *The tone of teaching*, explains pedagogy as "an attentive attunement of one's whole being to the child's experience of the world" (p. 49). Thoughtfulness, he argues, "is a special kind of knowledge" (p. 5), "a peculiar quality that has as much to do with what we are as what we do. It is a knowledge that issues from the heart as well as from the head" (p. 9).

Curriculum that is relevant and engaging for young people can be "negotiated" (Green, 2021) instead of prescribed; thereby focusing on students' lives and celebrating their successes rather than punishing failures (Smyth, 2018, p. 478). Slee (1997) explains why this is paramount:

> If pedagogy and curriculum fail to reach out to students to encourage learning rather than reaffirm failure, we amplify disaffection and disruption. If students are aware that schooling is leading them nowhere and that they have nothing to lose by being disruptive, we have very serious problems that challenge even the most assertive of behavioural management programs. (p. 8)

These "serious problems" are explained by Giroux (2012) as reform that has failed many young people because of a "pedagogy of technique and containment" (p. 68). Instead, Giroux (2012) asks us as educators to be public intellectuals and to "foster the conditions that enable students to think critically, take risks, and reflect on the knowledge they gain" (p. 68). This is a critical pedagogy that encourages students to be "informed citizens, workers and social agents" of the future (Giroux, 2012, p. 69). Hickey and Riddle (2023) agree that it is time to recognize the "informality of the pedagogical" and that the dynamics in classrooms should work to "recognise ways of speaking, of expressing opinion, and of moving about and using space that defy the 'rules'" (p. 10).

Simon (1992) outlines that pedagogy as "political practice" is risky "because it is neither neutral nor innocent" (p. 62). It is a "practice within which one acts with the intent of provoking experience that will simultaneously organize and disorganize a variety of understandings of our natural and social world" (p. 56). Nikolakaki (2012) poses provoking questions to express pedagogy as political practice:

> Pedagogy is not about the how of teaching; it is about the why. It forms the foundation of teaching, and it constitutes a basis for answering difficult questions or dilemmas of education: Why am I teaching? What is my scope or aim? How is knowledge selected? What are the consequences of my actions? Who benefits from this kind of education? Who gets left out? Am I really helping my students become adults who will be responsible and agents in society? (p. 24)

Rediscovering/Reclaiming the Relational

> Fostering student agency is an important component of a new educational narrative. (Reid, 2019, p. 285)

A new educational narrative or alternative to the neoliberal school is "grounded in a very different ideology, set of values, and sensibilities" (Smyth, 2018, p. 467) and fosters learning that emerges through relations and connections (Fielding & Moss, 2011, p. 27). Fitting into society is important for young people's identity and social development, and when these relations and connections are threatened then young people's focus is not on engaging in learning but on claiming status between friends in the classroom. This was expressed clearly by Max, one of the students I interviewed at Anchorage High:

> The other thing is if you stick up for someone you get a reputation. Yet, even if you are doing some of those little things, then you happen to be around a fight, even just looking, you get blamed for it, just because you have a reputation. That is something that happens at school, like last year I wasn't the best person in the school, sort of thing, and then I just did a few small things. But this year, because I have this reputation that they gave me, they pounce on me for the smallest things. (Interview with Max, July 2007)

Other students who participated in the second interview with Max also shared how important the camaraderie is between them as they defend their friends after what they perceive to be unjust decisions:

ES: Just like us sticking up for our friends when there is a fight or something. You stick up for your mates; they stick up for their mates.

KAI: If the kids in the class don't hear you stick up for yourself in class, they get really intimidating. But when you do say something to stick up for your rights, then the teacher gets narky, and says, "You're not coming back to my class."

MAX: If you incite it, you are the one who gets into trouble. You can't really complain because if the teacher feels like making a deal, then the other teachers will believe that story, not the students' version. (Interview with Es, Kai, and Max, August 2007)

As these young people expressed, if "the purposes of education are to assist [them . . .] to have the capacities to not only handle change but to *shape it*," then as educators we must "keep abreast of key societal changes" (Reid, 2019, p. 225, emphasis added).

Conclusion

> The principle of irrational authority based on power and exploitation must be replaced, not by a laissez-faire attitude, but by an authority which is based on the competence of knowledge and skill—not on intimidation, force, or suggestion. (Fromm, 1981/2010, n.p.)

> Hope of liberation does not mean liberation already. It is necessary to fight for it, within historically favourable conditions. (Freire, 1997, p. 12)

This chapter began with the significant work of Erich Fromm, who encourages us to challenge "the principle of irrational authority" of behavior and discipline policies and replace it with hope for an education based on "the presence of love: the depth of the relationship" (Fromm, 1956, p. 156). This is an education that is not only based on the competence of knowledge and skills but also "help[s] the child realize his [sic] potentialities" (Fromm, 1956, p. 186).

As Bauman (2006, p. 160) explains, it is our task (as the living) to keep this hope alive in a more loving, relational and just education. To keep the flame of hope alive, I have evoked Maxine Greene's (1995) vision of "releasing our imaginations," to bring the light back, and allow us to think of things as they *could* be as educators during neoliberal times. Throughout this chapter, as a way of bringing the vision of both "the light" and "the public" back in, I have drawn on Simon's (1992) "horizons of possibility" to reclaim spaces within education systems and policy formations. This is daring and complex work and will not happen without an impetus for new "education narratives," which must come from educators and school communities themselves (Reid, 2019, p. 303). It is time for educators to "take the lead if we are to reverse the years of damage" of neoliberal policy (Reid, 2019, p. 303).

A new education narrative must also be developed in partnership with those pedagogical directions and practices that engage young people in public schools as they reclaim the relational. These are authentic and nuanced "deeply contextualised enactments of teaching and learning" (Riddle & Hickey, 2023, p. 270), not the tokenistic and reductive "catch all" or "being in the service" notions of relationality (Riddle & Hickey, 2023, pp. 277–278) presently dominating student behavior and discipline policies and practices.

If education is to serve the public good, then educational policy making can be an important part of our democratic process (Reid, 2019, p. 150). This is a "radical democracy" allowing a "fluidity and contestation" to be embraced and placed in the foreground (Riddle, 2022, p. 8). Thus, the purpose of the next and final chapter is to embrace a radical democracy that is not only in the foreground but as Riddle (2022) explains, will continue to be sustainable into the future.

References

Ball, S. J. (1994). *Education reform: A critical and post-structural approach*. Open University Press.
Bauman, Z. (2006). *Liquid fear*. Polity Press.

Cook-Sather, A. (2002). Authorizing students' perspectives: Toward trust, dialogue, and change in education. *Educational Researcher, 31*(4), 3–14.
Darder, A. (2018). *The student guide to Freire's Pedagogy of the oppressed*. Bloomsbury.
Duncan-Andrade, J. M. R., & Morrell, E. (2008). *The art of critical pedagogy: Possibilities for moving from theory to practice in urban schools*. Peter Lang.
Fielding, M., & Moss, P. (2011). *Radical education and the common school: A democratic alternative*. Routledge.
Freire, P. (1992). *Pedagogy of hope*. Continuum.
Freire, P. (1997). *Pedagogy of the heart*. Continuum.
Freire, P. (2005). *Pedagogy of the oppressed* (M. B. Ramos, Trans.). Continuum. (Original work published 1970).
Fromm, E. (1956). *The art of loving*. Open Road Integrated Media.
Fromm, E. (1968). *The revolution of hope: Toward a humanized technology*. Bantam Books.
Fromm, E. (2010). *On disobedience: Why freedom means saying "no" to power*. Harper Collins E books. (Original work published 1981).
Giroux, H. A. (2003). Pedagogy of the depressed. In M. Peters, C. Lankshear, & M. Olssen (Eds.), *Critical theory and the human condition: Founders and praxis* (pp. 143–168). Peter Lang.
Giroux, H. A. (2012). *Education and the crisis of public values: Challenging the assault on teachers, students, and public education*. Peter Lang.
Green, B. (2021). Re-negotiating the curriculum? *Curriculum Perspectives, 41*, 213–225. https://doi.org/10.1007/s41297-021-00143-7
Greene, M. (1982). Public education and the public space. *Educational Researcher, 11*(6), 4–9.
Greene, M. (1995). *Releasing the imagination: Essays on education, the arts, and social change*. Jossey-Bass Publishers.
Greene, M. (2009). Teaching as possibility: A light in dark times. In S. Macrine (Ed.), *Critical pedagogy in uncertain times: Hope and possibilities* (pp. 136–149). Palgrave Macmillan.
Hickey, A., & Riddle, S. (2023). Proposing a conceptual framework for relational pedagogy: Pedagogical informality, interface, exchange and enactment. *International Journal of Inclusive Education*. Advance online publication. https://doi.org/10.1080/13603116.2023.2259906
Kelly, P., Campbell, P., & Howie, L. (2019). *Rethinking young people's marginalisation: Beyond neo-liberal futures?* Routledge.
Lawrence-Lightfoot, S., & Hoffmann Davis, J. (1997). *The art and science of portraiture*. Jossey-Bass.
Monbiot, G. (2017). *Out of the wreckage: A new politics for an age of crisis*. Verso.
Nikolakaki, M. (2012). Critical pedagogy in the new dark ages: Challenges and possibilities: An introduction. In M. Nikolakaki (Ed.), *Critical pedagogy in the new dark ages: Challenges and possibilities* (pp. 3–31). Peter Lang.
Reid, A. (2019). *Changing Australian education: How policy is taking us backwards and what can be done about it*. Allen & Unwin.
Riddle, S. (2022). *Schooling for democracy: Towards a more caring, inclusive and sustainable future*. Routledge.

Riddle, S., & Hickey, A. (2023). Reclaiming relationality in education policy: Towards a more authentic relational pedagogy. *Critical Studies in Education*, 64(3), 267–282. https://doi.org/10.1080/17508487.2022.2132414

Rizvi, F., & Lingard, B. (2010). *Globalizing education policies*. Routledge.

Senate, Education and Employment References Committee. (2023). *The issue of increasing disruption in Australian school classrooms: Interim report*. Commonwealth of Australia.

Senate, Education and Employment References Committee. (2024). *The issue of increasing disruption in Australian school classrooms: Final report*. Commonwealth of Australia.

Simon, R. I. (1992). *Teaching against the grain: Texts for a pedagogy of possibility*. Bergin & Garvey.

Slee, R. (1997, March). *Theorising discipline—Practical research implications for schools* [Paper presentation]. Annual meeting of the American Educational Research Association, Chicago.

Smyth, J. (2001). *Critical politics of teachers' work: An Australian perspective*. Peter Lang.

Smyth, J. (2018). The socially just school: Transforming young lives. In K. J. Saltman & A. J. Means (Eds.), *The Wiley handbook of global educational reform* (pp. 467–487). John Wiley & Sons.

Smyth, J., Angus, L., Down, B., & McInerney, P. (2009). *Activist and socially critical school and community renewal: Social justice in exploitative times*. Sense Publishers.

Stengers, I. (2002). A "cosmo-politics"—Risk, hope, change. In M. Zournazi (Ed.), *Hope: New philosophies for change* (pp. 244–272). Pluto Press.

Van Manen, M. (2002). *The tone of teaching: The language of pedagogy*. Althouse Press.

· 7 ·

CONCLUSION: SCHOOLING *FOR* DEMOCRACY (RIDDLE, 2022)

Introduction

As Reid (2019) explains, "approaches that exclude the voices of educators, students and parents" in education should be jettisoned (p. xxvi.). Kenway and Fahey (2009) agree that researchers need to be defiant, engaging, and provocative by "questioning received notions and creating new ways of seeing" (p. 14).

In the previous chapter, I called for a renewed educational narrative to reclaim the public, pedagogical, and relational. In this concluding chapter, I continue that line of argument and ask, if education is to serve the public good, then should not education policy making be an important part of our democratic process (Reid, 2019, p. 150)? What then does "schooling for democracy" look like?

It is the purpose of this closing chapter to navigate maps or constellations of activist and socially critical schools in communities (Smyth et al., 2009). Based on genealogical and ethnographic research data collated over a 30-year period from two secondary schools (Heron and Anchorage High), and the common key findings and themes collated from both case studies (Chapters 4 and 5), three framing topics emerge, which I will use to summarize and discuss schooling for democracy:

- being engaged in learning with young people via respect and compassion,
- establishing collaborative learning communities, and
- imagining a socially just school.

Being Engaged in Learning

Down and Choules (2017) argue "that students are more likely to engage in learning when they have ownership and control over what, how and with whom they learn" (p. 135). Young people "provide a powerful referent" and "offer a crucial index" (Giroux, 2011, p. 140) to measure societies' democratic values into the future.

A significant theme that emerged from the stories collected from both my field notes at Heron High and student interviews at Anchorage was the importance of being "engaged" by having one's teaching and learning needs met by both the school environment and a pedagogy of possibility (Simon, 1992). These needs include being offered respect and compassion.

Respect

As Smyth (2005) argues, "learning is a social process and having people around you who treat you with respect is crucial to student engagement and success" (p. 229). Sixteen-year-old Brad from Anchorage High explained:

> Sport is a good subject. Every Thursday I get to go surfing and body boarding at "The Point." I get to be out and about walking around the bush. There are not too many stupid rules, so it is a lot of fun and you don't get into trouble. The teacher gets into the water and has fun too. (Interview with Brad, August 2007)

In contrast, Smyth et al. (2004, p. 187) remind us, "students are often placed in situations where they have to consciously place on hold their personal views about respect, authority, dignity and fairness" when they themselves are not respected. Brad in his conversation with Jen, another student from Anchorage, gave examples of this:

BRAD: Some teachers scream to get your attention.
JEN: Mr. B just glares and makes noises and then takes you outside, very close to your head, tells you what to say.

BRAD: Then when he comes walking around, we pretend to be doing the right thing, and then we throw things when he is on the other side of the room.

JEN: The same with the phone. When he is away, we get ours out. Then when he is nearby, we put it away. So dumb.

BRAD: If we modelled our teachers, we would be the biggest brats in the world. For example, teachers scream, so you scream back. (Interview with Brad and Jen, July 2007)

Bessant et al. (2017) explain that "an authentic intergenerational contract involves dialogue," "listening to each other in conversation," and "coming to some degree of consensus about processes and content as well as disagreement" (p. 184). Consequently, when there is an absence of respect, listening, and consensus, students like Brad and Jen often disengage and easily fall back into a path of failure. Nora and Ev from Anchorage confirmed this:

NORA: For the teachers, they often think that we should respect them because they are our elders and stuff, but from a student's perspective, if they do not respect you, then why should you respect them?

EV: And sometimes they can be very disrespectful. (Interview with Nora and Ev, August 2007)

Ayers (2004) creates a comprehensive profile (below) to describe how the power of reciprocal respect can lead to greater engagement in learning for students like Nora and Ev:

> A primary challenge to teachers is to see each student as a three-dimensional creature, a person much like themselves, with hopes, dreams, aspirations, skills, and capacities; with a body and a mind and a heart and a spirit; with experience, history, a past, several possible pathways, a future. This knotty, complicated challenge requires patience, curiosity, wonder, awe, humility. It demands sustained focus, intelligent judgment, inquiry and investigation. It requires wide-awakeness, since every judgment is contingent, every view partial, and every conclusion tentative. The student is dynamic, alive, and forever in motion. Nothing is settled once and for all. No view is all views and no perspective every perspective. The student grows, and changes—yesterday's need is forgotten, today's claim is all-encompassing and brand-new. (p. 3)

Compassion

Rejecting schooling is nearly always a strongly emotional experience. (Furlong, 1991, p. 296)

Children are the heartbeat of politics. (Giroux, 2011, p. 140)

Although cultivating compassion in pedagogy cannot provide any assurance of social justice and democracy, it does create openings to impact youth and society in productive ways. (Zembylas, 2021, p. 815)

Smyth (2018), in describing a socially just school that has the capacity to transform young lives, details how emotionally demanding teaching is and how significant emotions are in enabling teachers to establish relations with their students: "through sympathy, interest, surprise, boredom, sense of humor, sometimes anger and annoyance" (p. 473). Carl, Tara, and Ev (from Anchorage High) shared the significance of solidarity based on emotion and respect in relationships with one another:

CARL: When we were in Year 7, a girl in our class was killed in a car accident. It was three years ago since her death last Tuesday,
ME: What did your school/class do to help you through that experience?
TARA: We planted a mulberry tree. It was raining that day, we were all around in a big circle, and there was a big tarp.
CARL: We had a big ceremony.
TARA: And a poem was read out . . . the tree is still there now.
CARL: That is because it has been fenced off.
TARA: It even has fruit on it.
EV: Everyone cried—I couldn't say anything; my throat was too dry.
CARL: Some of us were trying to make the others happy. They played her favorite songs on one of her favorite CDs, so many of us started singing.
TARA: She was a really good horse rider. Her friends brought her horse riding ribbons in. That made us even more upset.
EV: She had a page with a poem on it in our Year 7 graduation book. (Interview with Carl, Tara, and Ev, August 2007)

In this discussion, these students revealed the power and place of memories, emotions, and connections. This incident occurred three years prior to this interview and yet it still had a significant impact on them, and they wanted to share this memory with me as a significant other. This authentic social connection builds "pedagogies of compassion" (Zembylas, 2020, p. 255) which if nurtured could lead to "some sort of human connection between themselves and others" (Zembylas, 2020, p. 263). This is a very different pedagogy to the moralistic and sentimental discourse found in policies and procedures regarding student behavior (e.g., WADE, 2023) with an emphasis on the individual learning to "recognise and regulate their own emotions." This is the slippery discourse that becomes "empty, sliding signifiers [...] devoid of contextual meaning but reads nicely as a truism in policy" (Riddle & Hickey, 2023, p. 270).

A journal entry I wrote during the early stages of my ethnographic research at Anchorage High provides a sense of what teaching *for* and *with* compassion (Zembylas, 2020, p. 265) might be:

> Today I watched the joy experienced by teenagers playing in the surf. They were like young seal pups, free—excited, doing what they will. The sand glistened and the waves rolled ... The tide ebbed and flowed as it always does.
>
> I caught myself thinking about that freedom "being" and "doing" to express your authentic self—when experiencing that movement—that moment and what it means; something that matters.
>
> What made the day especially memorable was witnessing those kids "taking the day off school" yet being so in tune with nature and with each other and the world! I could not help but be caught up in their sense of adventure, expression and dare. That would have been hard to find between the grey walls of school that day. (Journal entry, March 4, 2006)

What is revealed here is the empathy I felt for these young people whose energy, excitement, and creativity I had witnessed as a teacher and researcher that day and how much it contrasted with the classrooms of confinement and conformity that many of these young people would have been escaping. Those classrooms were too often characterized by a focus on cognitive skills to improve performance in high-stakes tests; upholding the image of their school; lining up, hands up, heads down, being quiet, taking notes; all of which had little in common with the joy, fun, and freedom they were experiencing. Many students resent having to be passively obedient or face disciplinary consequences (Shor, 1992, p. 212).

In contrast, teaching with critical compassion necessitates establishing trust and developing "strong relationships with and among students" (Zembylas, 2020, p. 264). Smyth et al. (2008), during their extensive research into engaged learning, witnessed that the teachers who were passionate, committed, and respected by students were often those that "taught against the odds" and in "circumstances of diminishing resources" (p. 118).

Ultimately, "how students are enabled to relate to one another, to their teachers, school leaders and members of the community" (Smyth et al., 2008, p. 158) is what really matters in democratic schooling. It is "a hinge on which so many things open" (Hoffman, 2019, p. 249).

Collaborative Learning Communities

> Community is the place from which a new politics begins to grow. (Monbiot, 2017, p. 184)

The evolution and enactment of the Western Australian behavior and discipline policies (1998–2023) that have been investigated and discussed throughout this book demonstrate that they are "divorced" (Reid, 2019, p. 294) from the community they are intended to serve. The school community must be invited to collaborate in policy-making decisions if they are to be sustainable (Slee, 1992, pp. 194–195) because "the community has a sense of ownership of its schools," and therefore policy makers should be publicly accountable (Reid, 2019, p. 150).

This style of learning community is like an extended family (Tsiolkas, 2002, p. 108) because being involved in healthy relationships with others brings with it responsibility and commitment to the group. Rather than being on the outer, "all players," as Slee (1992) and Reid (2019) confirm, need to be involved, and not in a tokenistic manner, but genuinely and sincerely discussing, debating, inquiring; "offer[ing] means by which parents and students can be involved, sharing insights and experiences" (Reid, 2019, p. 294).

This is a process that will initially require "climbing out of the wreckage" (Monbiot, 2017). This takes time, patience, and perseverance; however, a respectful and authentic vision centered around the learning community itself can rebuild and revitalize community and "renew democracy and the hope invested in it" (Monbiot, 2017, p. 24). This type of community is a kind of mutual acceptance, not just tolerance. It is a learning community that understands without necessarily requiring consensus. As Hoffman (2019) reflects, community is "about coherence *despite* differences, finding common ground over which to move forward together" (p. 248).

This is very different to a school improvement and accountability culture of assessment and achievement in which "attendance and behaviour data (including suspension and exclusion data) will be important indicators of the health of the learning environment" (WADET, 2008, p. 8). In place of discourses shrouded in empty rhetoric throughout the school improvement regime, such as "being safe," "well managed," and "collecting data," Simon (1992) argues that authentic collaboration requires a sense of "collective venture, a learning together [...] something new is required of the student, an assessment of epistemological 'responsibleness'" (p. 65). He also argues that "a community of solidarity can neither be demanded, imposed, nor constructed; it can only be achieved" (p. 66).

Reid (2019) explains that education should evolve, not remain in a romantic past because "what constitutes a good education often changes from one context to the next" (p. x). A school with a vibrant learning community is more likely to encourage students to respect each other and their teachers, which in turn promotes the possibility of reciprocal learning. Collaborative learning communities, as described in this section, are important in connecting with and in establishing and maintaining a socially just school (Smyth et al., 2014).

Imagining a Socially Just School

The socially just school places students before the economy and regards disengagement as "a misdiagnosis of the issue" (Smyth, 2018). Instead, it ensures that the school curriculum, organization, and pedagogy is relevant, "connect[ing] to young people's lives and interests" (p. 481).

If education policy, including behavior management and discipline policy, "is to change direction, there is a need for a powerful alternative educational narrative that looks to the future and *trusts* the expertise of educators" (Reid, 2019, p. 151, emphasis added). The extensive multi-sited ethnographic research of Smyth et al. (2010), for example, after many conversations with numerous administrative staff, teachers, and students at four large government (public) secondary schools in Australia, unearthed interrelated themes that proved to be the most significant components in building a relational and socially just school. These components included:

- respectful relationships,
- flexible organizational features,
- student focused and supportive,
- pedagogy connected to students' lives (yet still challenging, rigorous, and fun),
- and the school valuing and including its communities (Smyth et al., 2010, pp. 200–206).

A relational and socially just school, as described by these scholars, will mean that "behaviour management is obviated" because the students themselves will be "active agents in constructing their own lives, rather than passive victims of other people's constructions" (Smyth, 2018, p. 483).

Summary

> The pressures and expectations and ferment of policy are enormous, but it cannot be assumed that there is a straightforward relationship between policy and practice. (Ball, 2021, p. 6)

My biggest hope is that this book tells a story that will activate change. We cannot keep doing discipline policy the way we presently are; "the pressures," the "expectations," and "ferment" of it, as Ball (2021) explains, are overwhelming, but "it cannot be assumed that there is a straightforward relationship" between this policy and the practices that happen in schools under the banner and guises of behavior management, safety, and wellbeing.

At the beginning of this book, I focused on my journey, awakening, and approach that led to my researching and "troubling" of school behavior and discipline policies in neoliberal times. I wrote about critical moments in my own life and teaching as a theoretical basis. By focusing on critical social theory and critical ethnography, I began to dismantle, interrupt, and challenge common-sense notions of behavior and discipline policies and practices that impact on many young people, their families, and their communities, especially those most disadvantaged.

To locate the broader policy landscape of troubling behavior and discipline policies, I posed questions; *What is neoliberalism? And where did it come from?* (Connell, 2013; Connell & Dados, 2014). This process led to an investigation of how neoliberal reform impacts on us all globally as "civic subjects" (Giroux, 2018) and understand why we become "consuming and marketable subjects" (p. 511). Throughout this chapter I shared the effects of neoliberal schooling on young people in particular to expose how it "militates against their interests" (Smyth, 2020, p. 686).

To gain understandings of how discipline policies and practices have evolved over time, Chapter 3 provided a significant historical context of contemporary behavior and discipline policies in tracing their origins from 16th-century Europe to 21st-century Australia. A genealogical approach served to unfold a series of recurring patterns and discourses, exposing those approaches, assumptions, and belief systems that lingered, many of which I critiqued as a conservative return to punishment practices.

In Chapters 4 and 5, I used "narrative agency" (Sennett, 2006, p. 188) to share the findings, understandings, and ethnographic evidence from the fields of two large government (public) secondary schools as case studies. These findings revealed that many schools in similar situations are experiencing neoliberal reform that relates to school effectiveness and school improvement policies that marginalizes and squeezes out too many. Using critical ethnography "bears witness" (Slee, 2011, p. 155) to the many injustices revealed throughout these chapters. Burawoy (2013) explains:

> We have to search for the most effective ramparts to reverse third-wave marketization. In that search the ethnographer plays a critical role, digging around like an archaeologist for the nuclei of contestation, for embryonic institutions struggling to make their appearance against the tsunami. We then have to comprehend the conditions for their expansion and dissemination. Ethnography is on the front-line in the battle to save society from market fundamentalism, so we had better reflect deeply on the fallacies to which it is prone. (pp. 534–535)

Bessant et al. (2017) argue that "one way of asking what we need to live a good life is to imagine a just society" in which "having both the freedom to choose and the ability to make real choice is justice" (p. 173). The ultimate purpose of the sixth chapter of this book was to make hope practical (McInerney, 2004) by disrupting and dismantling neoliberal school discipline policy from rhetoric to reform *for* social justice. Chapter 6 focuses on hope for transformation and seeks the relational rather than the fragmented, standardized, and measurable research often portrayed in Western worldviews (Markides, 2018, p. 293). This is a "relatedness that holds us in check, holds us up, holds us together" (Markides, 2018, p. 294). Throughout this chapter, I searched for a storyline in which the relational and relatedness could be considered authentic. The scholars I drew upon to do this work included Erich Fromm, John Smyth, Roger Simon, Paulo Freire, and Maxine Greene. These scholars, as Markides (2018) identifies, are "role models and teachers" (p. 298) whose ideas and theories assist in the search to generate new imaginings and narratives of hope for thinking and doing "otherwise" in schools.

Chapter 7 is a final activist and scholarly call for democratic schooling. It "views young people as a valuable resource" (Giroux, 2022, p. 29), provides teachers more say in what happens in their classrooms, places the public back into the sphere of education, and lays the foundation of a socialist democracy.

References

Ayers, W. (2004). *Teaching the personal and the political: Essays on hope and justice*. Teachers College Press.

Ball, S. (2021). *The education debate* (4th ed.). Policy Press.

Bessant, J., Farthing, R., & Watts, R. (2017). A new intergenerational contract. In J. Bessant, R. Farthing, & R. Watts (Eds.), *The precarious generation: A political economy of young people* (pp. 165–184). Routledge.

Burawoy, M. (2013). Ethnographic fallacies: Reflections on labour studies in the era of market fundamentalism. *Work, Employment and Society, 27*(3), 526–536.

Connell, R. (2013). The neoliberal cascade and education: An essay on the market agenda and its consequences. *Critical Studies in Education, 54*(2), 99–112.

Connell, R., & Dados, N. (2014). Where in the world does neoliberalism come from? The market agenda in southern perspective. *Theory & Society, 43*(2), 117–138. https://doi.org/10.1007/s11186-014-9212-9

Down, B., & Choules, K. (2017). Towards a pedagogy of personalisation: What can we learn from students? *Curriculum Perspectives, 37*, 135–145.

Furlong, V. J. (1991) Disaffected pupils: Reconstructing the sociological perspective. *British Journal of Sociology of Education, 12*(3), 293–307.

Giroux, H. A. (2011). *Zombie politics and culture in the age of casino capitalism*. Peter Lang.

Giroux, H. (2018). When schools become dead zones of the imagination: A critical pedagogy manifesto. In K. J. Saltman & A. J. Means (Eds.), *The Wiley handbook of global educational reform* (pp. 503–515). John Wiley & Sons.

Giroux, H. A. (2022). Cultural politics and the crisis of education and political agency. *Fast Capitalism, 19*(1), 17–33. https://doi.org/10.32855/fcapital.202201.002

Hoffman, J. (2019). *Irreplaceable: The fight to save our wild places*. Penguin Books.

Kenway, J., & Fahey, J. (2009). Imagining research otherwise. In J. Kenway & J. Fahey (Eds.), *Globalising the research imagination* (pp. 1–39). Routledge.

Markides, J. (2018). Reconciling an ethical framework for living well in the world of research. In J. Markides & L. Forsythe (Eds.), *Looking back and living forward: Indigenous research rising up* (pp. 291–300). Brill Sense.

McInerney, P. (2004). *Making hope practical: School reform for social justice*. Post Pressed.

Monbiot, G. (2017). *Out of the wreckage: A new politics for an age of crisis*. Verso.

Reid, A. (2019). *Changing Australian education: How policy is taking us backwards and what can be done about it*. Allen & Unwin.

Riddle, S. (2022). *Schooling for democracy: Towards a more caring, inclusive and sustainable future*. Routledge.

Riddle, S., & Hickey, A. (2023). Reclaiming relationality in education policy: Towards a more authentic relational pedagogy. *Critical Studies in Education, 64*(3), 267–282. https://doi.org/10.1080/17508487.2022.2132414

Sennett, R. (2006). *The culture of the new capitalism*. Yale University Press.

Shor, I. (1992). *Empowering education: Critical teaching for social change*. University of Chicago Press.

Simon, R. I. (1992). *Teaching against the grain: Texts for a pedagogy of possibility*. Bergin & Garvey.

Slee, R. (1992). Reforms and ravines: Diminishing risk in schools through systematic change. In R. Slee (Ed.), *Discipline in Australian public education: Changing policy and practice* (pp. 177–198). Australian Council for Educational Research.

Slee, R. (2011). *The irregular school: Exclusion, schooling, and inclusive education*. Routledge.

Smyth, J. (2005). Modernizing the Australian education workplace: A case of failure to deliver for teachers of young disadvantaged adolescents. *Education Review, 57*(2), 221–233.

Smyth, J. (2018). The socially just school: Transforming young lives. In K. J. Saltman & A. J. Means (Eds.), *The Wiley handbook of global educational reform* (pp. 467–487). John Wiley & Sons.

Smyth, J. (2020). A critical pedagogy of working class schooling. In S. Steinberg & B. Down (Eds.), *The Sage handbook of critical pedagogies* (pp. 681–693). Sage.

Smyth, J., Angus, L., Down, B., & McInerney, P. (2008). *Critically engaged learning: Connecting to young lives*. Peter Lang.

Smyth, J., Angus, L., Down, B., & McInerney, P. (2009). *Activist and socially critical school and community renewal: Social justice in exploitative times*. Sense Publishers.

Smyth, J., Down, B., & McInerney, P. (2010). *"Hanging in with kids" in tough times: Engagement in contexts of educational disadvantage in the relational school*. Peter Lang.

Smyth, J., Down, B., McInerney, P., & Hattam, R. (2014). *Doing critical educational research: A conversation with the research of John Smyth*. Peter Lang.

Smyth J., & Hattam, R., with Cannon, J., Edwards, J., Wilson, N., & Wurst, S. (2004). *Dropping out, drifting off, being excluded: Becoming somebody without school*. Peter Lang.

Tsiolkas, C. (2002). On believing. In M. Zournazi (Ed.), *Hope: New philosophies for change* (pp. 98–121). Pluto Press.

WA Department of Education (WADE). (2023). Student behaviour in public schools policy.

WA Department of Education and Training (WADET). (2008). School improvement and accountability framework.

Zembylas, M. (2020). Critical pedagogies of compassion. In S. R. Steinberg & B. Down (Eds.), *The Sage handbook of critical pedagogies* (pp. 254–267). Sage.

Zembylas, M. (2021). Adorno on democratic pedagogy and the education of emotions: Pedagogical insights for resisting right-wing extremism. *Policy Futures in Education, 19*(7), 809–825.

INDEX

activism 2–5, 10–13, 38, 115, 123
Angus, Lawrence 73, 76
Angus, Max 48, 52–53
Apple, Michael W. 8, 10, 23, 63, 74
Araújo, Marta 55
Aronowitz, Stanley 10, 31
Australian Child and Adolescent Survey on Mental Health and Wellbeing 30
Australian Curriculum 24, 27, 109
Australian Curriculum, Assessment and Reporting Authority 27
Australian Institute of Teaching and School Leadership 49
Australian Law Reform Commission 29
Ayers, William 5, 30, 117

Ball, Stephen J. 4, 7, 11–12, 23, 37, 53, 65, 103, 122
Bauman, Zygmunt 75, 105, 112
behavior and discipline policies
 and Christianity 40–41, 50
 and psychology 21, 42
 behavior centers 29, 31, 51–54

behavior management plans 67, 84–86, 93
classroom management skills 49, 67
codes of conduct 70, 87, 94
corporal punishment 42–45
deficit thinking 12, 20, 29, 30–33, 46 55–56
"disruptive" students 45, 48, 55, 69, 71
education entrepreneurs 50, 74
history 13, 33, 37–48, 52–57, 98, 122
impact on young people 7, 12, 73, 81, 96, 122
in colonial Australia 41
inclusion centers 28
isolation rooms 46–47, 54–55
moral education 41, 44, 50, 53
obedience 40, 52–53, 57, 87, 93
pathologizing discourses 29, 54, 56, 75, 97–98
suspension and exclusion 44–47, 67, 83, 87, 96, 120
zero tolerance 20, 28–31, 96–97
"Behaviour Curriculum" 27, 109

INDEX

Behaviour Management and Discipline Strategy 49, 67
Bennett, Barrie 49, 67
Bennett, Tom 50
Berndtsson, Kristina Hunehäll 97
Bessant, Judith 39, 92, 117, 123
Biddulph, Steve 38
Bloch, Ernst 106
Burawoy, Michael 20, 123

Caldwell, Brian 66
Chilie 24
Chomsky, Noam 87
Choules, Kathryn 11, 32, 116
Connell, Raewyn 1, 12, 22–25, 31, 41, 63, 73, 88, 95, 98, 122
Cook-Sather, Alison 96, 103
Cottle, Michelle 11, 12
critical moments 3–9, 122
critical theory 2, 9, 10, 11, 122
Cuttance, Peter 66

Dados, Nour 12, 22, 23, 31, 122
De Jong, Terry 48
democracy 7–8, 14, 112, 115, 123
Dewey, John 10, 93
Down, Barry 3, 5, 11, 30–32, 66, 97, 116

Ecclestone, Kathryn 50–51
education
    and communities 32–33, 120–122
    and democracy 115, 121
    and public good 73, 108, 112, 115
    and relationships, importance of 14, 20, 103–112, 123
education policy
    reform of 12, 21, 65, 72–73
    see also behavior and discipline policies, neoliberalism, schools, Western Australia
Ellsworth, Jeanne 90, 94
England 24, 27, 31, 41
ethnography
    critical ethnography 11, 13, 64, 122–123

critical policy ethnography 2, 11–13, 64, 83, 122–123
    recruitment of participants 84–86
Europe 32, 39–42, 52–53, 56, 66, 122

Fahey, Johannah 7, 115
Fielding, Michael 11, 14, 28, 74, 110
Fine, Michelle 31–32, 75
Fogelgarn, Rochelle Karen 53
Freire, Paulo 1–6, 10–11, 14, 19–20, 57, 96–98, 103–104, 106, 111, 123
Fromm, Erich 2, 8, 14, 32, 104, 111–112, 123
Fullan, Michael 49
genealogy 13, 33, 37–39, 57, 64, 76, 115, 12

Germany 27
Gibson, Rex 9, 10
Gillies, Val 10, 29–31, 54
Giroux, Henry A. 1, 9–14, 21–23, 32, 37–38, 57, 107–110, 116, 118, 122–123
Glasser, William 45, 48
Good Standing Policy 71, 83, 86–91, 94
Gorski, Paul C. 29
Greene, Maxine 10, 11, 14, 104, 106, 108, 112, 123
Groundwater-Smith, Susan 38
Gunter, Helen 9, 10, 14, 66

Hall, G. Stanley 38
Harber, Clive 41, 53
Hargreaves, Andy 68, 70
Hattam, Rob 7, 11, 98, 99
Haywood, Chris 10
Hickey, Andrew 14, 103–104, 107, 110, 112, 119
Hoffman, Julian 119, 120
hope
    critical 104–105
    transformative 11, 104
Hyde, Norman 44

imagination 8, 11, 32, 104–107
Ingram, Eirlys 51–52

Kearney, Alison 56–57
Kelly, Peter James 98, 106
Kenway, Jane 6, 7, 11, 115
Kincheloe, Joe L. 10, 21
Knight, Tony 21, 24
Kress, Tricia M. 5, 9, 10, 22

La Boétie, Étienne de 40, 52
Ladson-Billings, Gloria 25, 89, 94
Latour, Bruno 38–39
Lawrence, David 30
Leistyna, Pepi 14, 21
Lewis, Ramon 53
Lewis, Tim 71–72
Lillico, Ian 38
Lingard, Bob 25, 27
Luke, Carmen 39

Mac an Ghaill, Mairtin 10, 64
Madison, D. Soyini 82
Maguire, Meg 67–70, 73, 76
marginalization 10, 64, 94
    see also Young People and marginalization
Markides, Jennifer 123
McDonald, Tim 49
McInerney, Peter 11, 24, 123
Meier, Deborah 11, 95
Mercier, Jean-Pierre 64
Meredyth, Denise 13, 38
Mills, C. Wright 20
Mills, Martin 10, 31
Monbiot, George 106–108, 120
Morris, Marla Beth 39
Moss, Peter 11, 14, 28, 74, 110
Multi-Tiered Implementation Support (MTIS) 64, 72, 76, 108

National Assessment Program—Literacy and Numeracy (NAPLAN) 48
neoliberalism
    and individualism 23, 25, 28
    impact on young people 2, 7, 12, 22, 31, 73, 96, 122

    in schools 4, 20–28
    neoliberal policy reforms 4, 21, 22, 29
    resistance to 7, 14, 19, 108
New Zealand 24, 26
Nikolakaki, Maria 21, 23, 110

Organisation for Economic Co-operation and Development (OECD) 20, 25–28, 49

Paul, William 23
pedagogy
    alienating 28, 40–41, 90, 96, 118
    critical 1, 2, 9–11, 21–22, 110
    engaging 110, 118, 121
    of compassion 10, 107, 116–119
    pedagogy of possibility 4, 10, 116
Pedagogy of the oppressed 2, 104
performativity 3, 8, 54, 66–67, 73–74, 87, 92–93
Pini, Barbara 10, 31
Pipeline Project 48, 52
political awakening 2, 8–11, 20–23, 82, 107, 110, 122
Positive Behavior Support (PBS) school 7, 48, 64, 71–76, 108
positivism 4, 22–24, 72
Programme for International Student Assessment (PISA) 27, 48
Protestantism 39, 41

Reay, Diane 10, 24, 26, 31
Reid, Alan 11, 14, 74, 106–115, 120–121
Riddle, Stewart 14, 103–104, 107, 110, 112, 115, 119
Rizvi, Fazal 23, 27, 109
Robinson, Ken 3
RYPPLE 64, 71–72, 76

Sahlberg, Pasi 20, 24, 26, 27
Saltman, Kenneth J. 70, 96
schools
    high-stakes testing 25, 27–28
    Individual Education Plans 48, 94
    privatization 26, 49

relationally engaging 121
school choice 24
socially just 116, 118, 121–122
School Development Plan (SDP) 46, 64, 66
Senate Education and Employment References Committee 27, 28, 55, 109
Serres, Michel 38–39
Shor, Ira 9, 93, 119
Simon, Roger I. 4, 10, 14, 105–106, 109–110, 116, 120, 123
Slee, Roger 13, 27–28, 30, 33, 39, 42, 44, 54, 56, 71, 89, 109, 120, 123
Smilanich, Peter 49, 67
Smith, Bruce 11
Smith, Kersha 31–32, 75
Smyth, John 7, 10–14, 21–30, 33, 65, 67, 73, 87, 92–99, 105–106, 109–110, 115–116, 118–119, 121–123
Spinks, Jim 66
State School Teachers' Union of WA 49, 67
Steinberg, Shirley 5–7
Stengers, Isabelle 106
Stevenson, Robert B. 90, 94
Student Information System (SIS) 47, 53, 70, 75, 84
Students at Risk program 29
surveillance 30, 39, 41, 53, 74, 83, 86, 90–91
Sweden 24, 56, 72

Tamboukou, Maria 13, 37
Taylor, Emmeline 13, 56, 57
teachers
    and neoliberal reform 12, 29, 45–46, 53, 73, 74
    deskilling 8
    labor 49, 67, 91
    silencing of 6, 67–68, 73, 85
    student-teacher relationships 3, 32, 83, 88–90, 92–95, 98–99, 103, 105, 111, 116–121
    work 11, 66, 69, 77
Thériault, Virginie 64
Torres, Carlos Alberto 10
Tyler, Deborah 3, 38

United Kingdom 50, 66, 109
United States 24, 27, 38, 42, 52, 66, 97

Van Heertum, Richard 10
Van Manen, Max 73, 109

Weaver, John A. 39
Welch, Anthony 24, 81
Western Australia
    Beazley Report 44, 45
    behavior centers 45, 51
    Behaviour Management Policy 46
    Chaplaincy in Schools program 44
    Curriculum and Re-engagement in Education (CARE) schools 51–52, 54, 92
    Dettman Report 44, 55
    Louden Report 45, 55
    School Education Act 1999 (WA) 45, 46
    uniform policy 70
Whitty, Geoff 87
Wrigley, Terry 10, 25, 28, 65

young people
    and hope 32, 104–105, 107
    and identity 56, 88, 95, 98, 111
    and marginalization 7, 25, 33, 51, 87, 92, 96–97, 110
    and poverty 25, 29
    exclusion of 92–93
    listening to 81, 94, 98, 119
    media misrepresentation of 96–97
    pathologization 29, 31, 38, 52, 55–56
    relationships, importance of 85, 95, 107, 112, 116
    speaking back 82
    see also behavior and discipline policies and impact on young people
    see also neoliberalism and impact on young people

Zembylas, Michalinos 10, 118–19
Zhang, Maverick 19–20
Zinn, Howard 65

Studies in Criticality

Series Editor
Shirley R. Steinberg

Counterpoints publishes the most compelling and imaginative books being written in Education and Cultural Studies today. Grounded on the theoretical advances in critical theory, feminism, and postcolonialism in the last two decades of the twentieth century, Counterpoints engages the meaning of these innovations in various forms of educational expression. Committed to the proposition that theoretical literature should be accessible to a variety of audiences, the series insists that its authors avoid esoteric and jargonistic languages that transform educational scholarship into an elite discourse for the initiated. Scholarly work matters only to the degree it affects consciousness and practice at multiple sites. The editorial policy of *Counterpoints* is based on these principles and the ability of scholars to break new ground, to open new conversations, to go where educators have never gone before.

For additional information about this series or for the submission of manuscripts, please contact:

>Shirley R. Steinberg, Series Editor
>msgramsci@gmail.com

To order other books in this series, please contact our Customer Service Department:

>peterlang@presswarehouse.com (within the U.S.)
>orders@peterlang.com (outside the U.S.)

Or browse online by series:

>www.peterlang.com

www.ingramcontent.com/pod-product-compliance
Lightning Source LLC
Chambersburg PA
CBHW061719300426

44115CB00014B/2750